CHARACTER QUEST

VOLUME ONE

STUDENT EDITION

Authors

SHARON R. BERRY, Ph.D., and OLLIE E. GIBBS, Ed.D.

LifeWay®

Published by
LifeWay Christian School Resources
One LifeWay Plaza
Nashville, TN 37234

Created and Developed by

Christian Academic Publications and Services, Inc.
Birmingham, Alabama

ISBN: 0-7673-3480-5
Dewey Decimal Classification: 248.82
Subject Heading: CHRISTIAN LIFE--TEXTS \ BIBLE--TEXTS

CharacterQuest, Volume One: Student Edition

To order additional copies of this resource: WRITE LifeWay Christian Resources Customer
Service, One LifeWay Plaza, Nashville, TN 37234-0113; FAX order to (615) 251-5933;
PHONE 1-800-458-2772; EMAIL to CustomerService@Lifeway.com.

CharacterQuest, Volume 1

Table of Contents

INTRODUCTION

Who are you—way down deep inside where no one can see? What things are of greatest importance to you? To whom are you most committed? What is your nature and being? What are some things you would do, or not do, no matter the pressure given by others? What are you really like when no one is looking? All of these questions relate to the word "character."

The word "character" is defined as a distinguishing mark or distinctive quality. The sum of many of these unique traits defines the character of a person—who that person really is.

Name a person you know, perhaps a Jonathan or Rebecca. You immediately think about that person's looks and personality. These are the features you can see in their appearance and behavior. However, if asked to describe someone's character, you would have to think deeper into what features are consistently shown in that person's life. Is Jonathan likely to cheat if given an opportunity, or can you really depend on him to be honest no matter what happens? Does Rebecca's voice always sound a sour note, or is she basically cheerful and encouraging to others? The internal qualities that you observe daily in your friends make up their character. At the same time, the qualities they see in you every day define your character.

Who are you, really, way deep inside? Now is a good time to think about how others might describe you and how you might describe yourself. Look at the words in the following lists. Circle the top five positive traits you feel are generally true, or are likely to be said by others, about you.

kind	mature	hurtful to others
understanding	forgiving	impatient
truthful	cooperative	disorganized
sincere	self-disciplined	always late
courageous	persevering	undependable
loyal	prayerful	not a promise keeper
friendly	committed to Christ	not conscientious
respectful	shows initiative	unreliable
considerate	respectful	disobedient
joyful	orderly	always teasing
hard-working	careful	a show-off
conscientious	able to lead others	poor judgment
obedient	honest	immature
loving	prompt and on time	doesn't finish things
humble	selfish	prideful
tolerant	controlling	boastful
peaceable	unthankful	tattles
tender-hearted	hypocritical	gossips
determined	holds grudges	thinks sin is fun
wise	dishonest	wants to be first
generous	lazy	treats others unfairly
responsible	careless	selfish
merciful	untrustworthy	foolish
helpful	cheats	jealous
caring	cranky	insensitive
patient	never satisfied	stirs up trouble
faithful	complaining	gives up quickly
thankful	not a team player	argumentative
reverent	rude	

Obviously, these lists do not include everything, but they give you a good idea of the subject of this course: *CharacterQuest*. Your character is what you are when no one is looking. It is your inner heart from which all your personality and behaviors flow. Take a moment to read and write out the verse below.

Luke 6:45

_____

_____

_____

_____

_____

As a young teen, you are becoming more and more the person you want to be. Your parents' influence and control will lessen during these years as you decide what issues really matter to you. You are in the process of building the character which will in many ways determine the rest of your life.

Character really is important! It matters in the way you perceive yourself and the feelings you have about yourself. It is important with your parents, determining how much they can trust you and thus give you privileges to go and do things on your own. It counts with your teachers as they make assignments and give grades. And it matters with your friends! Are you loyal and caring? Can you be depended upon when trouble comes? Most importantly, character is significant with God! Are you becoming the person He wants you to be?

It is not unusual to pick up a newspaper and find stories on college students cheating, a local political leader caught in a lie, a congressman leading an impure life or even the head of a Christian organization stealing millions of dollars. Hot topics of conversation often focus on morality crises, ethical dilemmas and deteriorating societal values. Some people blame the government; others blame television. Teachers blame parents, and parents blame teachers. All agree that things must change dramatically with the next generation (that means you and your friends). All agree that character matters in the world today.

For example, employers seeking workers to place in good jobs with high salaries made the following comments about young people and why they were not successful in business:

> They are not dependable; they cannot take suggestions; they do not cooperate. If they finish one job, they expect someone to find them another instead of finding it for themselves. They are not punctual; they arrive late and begin to look at the clock before closing time. They are not loyal, criticizing and condemning unwisely and unjustly. They are untidy in their personal appearance.

All of these reasons relate to the character of individuals, not how smart they are or how much they know. Thus, good character is vital for your future.

The topics of ethics, morals, values and character are not new in education. Many notable people supported character education. Noah Webster, author of the first dictionary published in America, was a very committed Christian who greatly influenced our government. You can probably find a *Webster's Dictionary* in your classroom or library (greatly revised from the original one). It was Mr. Webster who said:

> In my view, the Christian religion is the most important and one of the first things in which all children, under a free government, ought to be instructed. The moral principles and precepts contained in the Scriptures ought to form the basis of all our civil constitutions and laws. All miseries and evils which men suffer from (the vice, crime, ambition, injustice, oppression, slavery and war) proceed from their despising or neglecting the precepts contained in the Bible.

Mr. Webster wrote a series of lessons entitled *Advice to the Young and Moral Catechism.* In them he spoke of obedience, love, curiosity of nature, faith, holiness, justice, service, humility, generosity, truth, gratitude, cheerfulness, industry and many other characteristics that were aimed at "learning those things which are to make you good citizens, useful members of society, and candidates for a happy state in another world (Heaven)."

Another name you will recognize is Benjamin Franklin. Remember that he discovered electricity by flying a kite in a storm. He was also a main figure in the first conventions in Philadelphia which framed the Constitution of the United States. When others could not agree and threatened to disband and go home to the colonies, Mr. Franklin proposed a day of prayer. God used him greatly to influence the foundations of government in the United States.

Benjamin Franklin is also well known for his efforts to establish a public school for common people who could not afford the elite private education of his day. The emphasis of this school was on the development of moral character. In fact, the teachers and principal met many months and concluded that, while subject matter was very important and desirable, character development was most needful. The virtues included were "unselfishness, self-control, honesty, economy, thrift, orderliness, the ability to reconcile differences, the ability to direct intelligently and cheerfully, an appreciation of art and beauty, and, most of all, a loving disposition, which is able to stand under many tests." Many schools based on the original model established by Benjamin Franklin are still in existence today.

A more current name you will recognize is Charles Lindbergh. He is famous for flying the first plane across the Atlantic Ocean. His comments demonstrate that he understood the importance of strong character.

> *I came to the conclusion that if I knew the difference between the right way to do a thing and the wrong way to do it, it was up to me to train myself to do the right thing at all times. So I drew up a list of character factors. At night I would read off my list of character factors, and those which I had fulfilled satisfactorily during the day I would mark*

with a red cross. Those I had not been called upon to demonstrate that day would get no mark. But those character factors which I had actually violated each day, I would mark with a black cross. I began to check myself from day to day to compare my blacks and reds from month to month and year to year. I was glad to notice an improvement as I grew older.

Here are the "character factors" that Lindbergh recorded.

altruism	no sarcasm
ambition	no fault-finding
brevity in speech	no talking about others
concentration	no talking too much
calmness in temper	optimism
clean body	perseverance
clean speech	physical exercise
clean conduct	pleasant voice
cheerfulness	punctuality
courage	patience
courtesy	politeness
decisiveness	respect supervisors
determination	respect fellowman
economy	readiness to compromise
energy	recreation: manful not sinful
enthusiasm	self-esteem
firmness	self-control
faith	self-confidence
gracefulness	sense of humor
hopefulness	sleep and rest
industry	sympathy
justice	sincerity
moderateness	tact
modesty	thoroughness
neat appearance	unselfishness
no argument	

Character counted to many famous people as they achieved success in our world. Does character count for you?

Because moral values and character issues are of such concern in the world today, many businesses, colleges and schools have designed courses in which their employees or students study the development of these traits. Most of these courses have no Biblical basis for their subject matter. They simply say that fairness, truthfulness, concern for others, honesty, etc., are good for society. Therefore, people can learn the right thing and be motivated to do the right thing apart from any particular religion—especially one founded on the Bible. History has proven these thoughts wrong. Education can make a difference in the head of mankind but not in the heart of mankind.

A heart change is necessary if a person is to develop good character and live justly in the world. This is the meaning of 2 Corinthians 5:17: "Therefore, if anyone is in Christ, he is a new creation; old things have passed away; behold, all things have become new." From this change of heart and commitment to live in a new relationship with Jesus Christ, a person begins the process of Romans 12:2: "And do not be conformed to this world, but be transformed by the renewing of your mind, that you may prove what is that good and acceptable and perfect will of God."

Does this mean only Christians can develop good character? No, not at all. Some people using the name of Christ (Hitler, for one) have caused great harm in the world. On the other hand, many people live morally good lives in comparison to others (remember the rich young ruler). However, it is only the Christian who has a deep commitment to God, believes the Bible has given us everything we need for godliness and life, and has the Holy Spirit as a helper in conforming to the character of Jesus Christ.

All admirable character traits have their ultimate source and example in God, Who is the Father of Light and Giver of every good and perfect gift. As we accept His Son Jesus, and He begins to live His life in us, the character traits begin to naturally occur. They are not forced on us like an old coat that is too tight and heavy. Rather, they begin to grow within us as we daily commit ourselves to cooperate with the Holy Spirit. He teaches, leads, convicts and gives victory. This is a wonderful experience.

Character matters! This course has been designed to help you study this very important topic. It is one of two courses for your age group which focus on the development of admirable character. Each week you will consider a different character trait. You will study Biblical examples, definitions, and most important, you will learn how to include each character trait in your life. Hopefully, you will commit to learning as much as you can. But head knowledge is not the goal of your study. Your application of godly principles to everyday life is really the test of success. May God bless you as you follow the prescription of Peter.

"Giving all diligence, add to your faith virtue, to virtue knowledge, to knowledge self-control, to self-control perseverance, to perseverance godliness, to godliness brotherly kindness, and to brotherly kindness love. For if these things are yours and abound, you will be neither barren nor unfruitful in the knowledge of our Lord Jesus Christ." (2 Peter 1:5–8)

Inquiry-Action Intro.1

2 Peter 1:5-7

Start with _____

With _____ (or hard work)

add _____.

Then add _____,

_____,

_____,

_____,

_____ _____,

and _____.

INQUIRY-ACTION Intro.2

A LETTER TO ME

Date: _____

Dear _____,

After giving it some thought, the three character areas I would like to work on during this course are _____,
_____, and _____.
I believe I can do this in the following ways:

_____

_____

_____

_____

_____

_____

_____

_____

_____

With commitment to myself alone,

_____

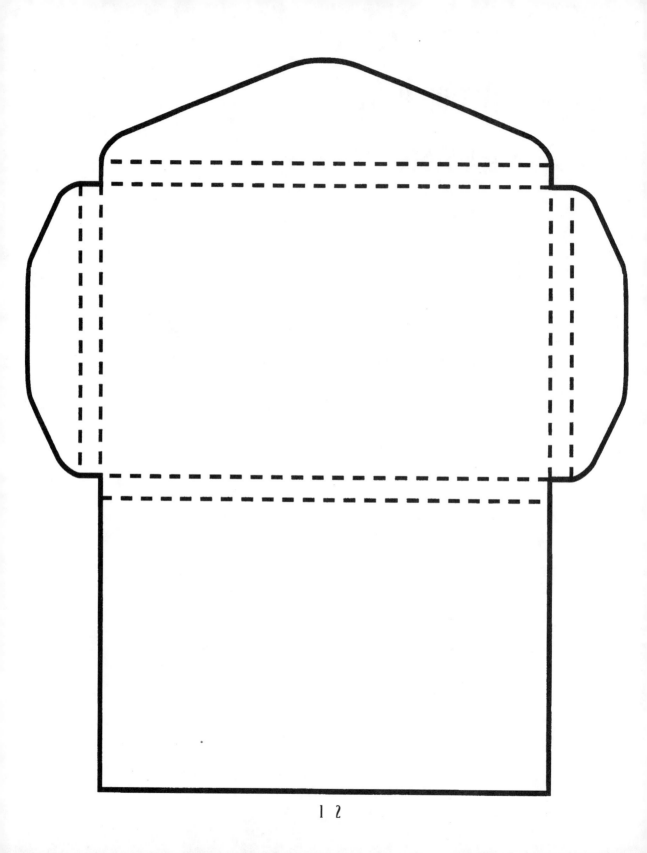

12

INQUIRY-ACTION Intro.3

CHARACTER SEARCH

```
Y T I L I M U H M R Y R X S S R E V E R E N C E M M G L A F
L N I N T E G R I T Y J K S E S W K B G C O M M I T M E N T
L O Q G V Q W X G O F W E E S R W I A P U R I T Y X V G T V
S E L F C O N T R O L N A E L N V R S L O V E A J J T N N C
J S F Y U V A E R T L L N F G B U I O D R K L S C H B Y E O
X Y S W C Y C G E U S E J F T O M E C E O E D J A E Z T M N
V L D V V N I N F H V S S K C K C N V E C M S N T T W I T T
V B Z D E V G Y N I R T E I I O D O U I K N K P K S V L N R
I V M I E L O H T O H V W N N O U I E B T F E L E B H I E O
N S T N N J M N S H F L D F I C F T Y T U A P I U C X B T L
V A E A Q E E V W M M N I Y C L E A V L M Y I B D B T I N L
P S I Q H T I A F U E D P W A D R R N Z L T H T T E I S O E
S H J V T F Y K K S E K N P V B H E I U O I S R I O B N C D
C H J A U C T A S N R E Y A R P S P D T S R R W A N Y O U S
K Z C J Z C L G C J X F O M G S U O J R Y U E I R M I P N P
J S F D O O A E D I L I G E N C E O F Y O T D G X E J S O E
M H K P R B Y M B Y T N E M N R E C S I D A A Y S V A E X E
G B O Y M Y O V M S Q H Z H O N E S T Y S M E R B A P R V C
P Y N F F Y L E N C O U R A G E M E N T J L L N N F G R T H
```

LOVE	LOYALTY	DISCERNMENT
WISDOM	HUMILITY	SINCERITY
OBEDIENCE	ORDERLINESS	PURITY
COURAGE	CONFIDENCE	MATURITY
ATTENTIVENESS	DILIGENCE	CONTROLLED SPEECH
FAITH	PRAYER	KINDNESS
RESPONSIBILITY	INTEGRITY	RESPECT
THANKFULNESS	PATIENCE	LEADERSHIP
HONESTY	FORGIVENESS	COMMITMENT
JOYFULNESS	INITIATIVE	SERVICE
SELF-CONTROL	CONTENTMENT	REVERENCE
	ENCOURAGEMENT	

LOVE

The Foundational Character Trait

> *"A dream is a wish your heart makes, when you're fast asleep. In dreams you will lose your heartaches; whatever you wish for, you keep. Have faith in your dreams and someday your rainbow will come sliding through. No matter how your heart is grieving—if you keep on believing—a dream that you wish will come true."*

Do you recognize the words above? Here's a hint. They are the words of a song from a very popular fairy tale movie. Can you think of the name of that story? If you guessed Cinderella, you're right!

The story of Cinderella has all of the characteristics of a fairy tale love story. There is a beautiful palace and all of the splendor of a kingdom. There is a handsome prince, heir to the throne, who is looking for a wife. And, of course, there is Cinderella. Although she is kind, beautiful and pure in heart, she is also poor and unfairly treated by her stepmother and stepsisters.

The stepmother does everything she can to keep Cinderella from fulfilling her dreams. First, she tries to keep Cinderella from attending the ball at the palace. But she fails. Then, when the prince's servant is looking for the maiden who can wear the glass slipper, the stepmother once again intervenes. She refuses to let Cinderella try on the slipper, hoping that it will fit one of her own daughters.

In spite of all the obstacles she faces, Cinderella is finally given the opportunity to prove that the missing glass slipper belongs to her. She is the one the prince has been seeking. The prince and Cinderella are married and, as the story goes, "lived happily ever after." Cinderella's dream, the words of the opening song of the story, has finally come true. Unfortunately, too many people think of love in terms of a fairy tale. But love is more than romance, a walk in the moonlight and living "happily ever after." Love is meeting the needs of someone else, unselfishly.

Suppose you are assigned to write a report on the topic of love. As you begin your research, you will quickly learn that there are two types of love: conditional and unconditional. Further research reveals that there are two types of conditional love. There is the IF type of love and the BECAUSE type of love. Let's take a minute to look at the difference between these two types of conditional love.

Have any of your classmates ever said that they would be your friend if you did what they wanted you to do? Sometimes what they wanted you to do was harmless, like giving up that special dessert you had in your lunch. There are other times when you might be asked to do very dangerous, or even illegal, things to gain their friendship.

This is an example of the first type of conditional love. This kind of love says "I will love you IF you do what I want you to do." It is not real love when you are required to earn the love (or friendship) of others by doing what they request. You can be sure that this type of relationship will last only as long as you are able, or willing, to do what you're asked.

The most common type of conditional love focuses on what you look like, who your friends are or what you have. This type of love might be described as, "I love (or like) you BECAUSE you are attractive." Or, "I love (or like) you BECAUSE you are popular."

If you will just take a moment to think about the students in your school, you will quickly realize that the relationships between many of these students centers around this BECAUSE type of conditional love. Think about your relationships with your friends. Do you love (or like) them IF they do things for you or BECAUSE they look a certain way or have certain things? Conditional love is not the type of love described in the Bible.

Unconditional love says "I love you PERIOD." "I love you no matter what!" This is the type of love that everyone really wants. Everyone wants to feel secure in the knowledge that, no matter what happens, true friends will not desert them.

The greatest example of unconditional love is represented by the Lord Jesus Christ when He died on the Cross for our sins. Jesus chose to give Himself as a sacrifice for our sins. His act of love is explained in the following passages of Scripture:

> **We are all sinners.** "For all have sinned and fall short of the glory of God" (Romans 3:23).

> **Death comes as a result of our sins.** "For the wages of sin is death" (Romans 6:23a).

> **Eternal life comes through Jesus Christ.** ". . . the gift of God is eternal life in Christ Jesus our Lord" (Romans 6:23b).

> **The love of Jesus was demonstrated on the cross.** "And being found in appearance as a man, He humbled Himself and became obedient to the point of death, even the death of the cross." (Philippians 2:8).

Unconditional love is what Jesus expects of each of us. Jesus wants us to unselfishly meet the needs of others. Are there students in your school who seem to have no friends? Unconditional love means that you take the initiative to become their friends. Are there families in your community who lack sufficient food or clothing? If your life is characterized by unconditional love, you will want to find ways to help these families obtain the food or clothing that they need.

A number of years ago there was a popular song with the following words: "What the world needs now is love, sweet love." It is true that we do need more love in this world. But we don't need the IF and BECAUSE types of conditional love. What is needed is unconditional love. We need to begin by accepting the unconditional love of Jesus Christ and the salvation that He has provided for us. Then each of us needs to daily practice unconditional love in our lives as we seek to unselfishly meet the needs of others.

INQUIRY-ACTION 1.1

LOVE IS . . .

1. What is conditional love?

_____

_____

2. What are two words often used in conditional love?

_____

_____

3. Describe an example of conditional love from your experience, a current news story or from the Bible.

_____

_____

4. What is unconditional love?

_____

_____

5. What is a Biblical example of this kind of love?

_____

_____

6. Are there some people who love you unconditionally—meaning that they would love you no matter what? Write some of their initials.

_____

_____

7. Why is it hard for people to love unconditionally?

_____

_____

8. Will you make a promise to begin learning how to love others unconditionally? _____

INQUIRY-ACTION 1.2

For each characteristic in 1 Corinthians 13:4-8a, explain or give an example of Loving (focused on others) and Unloving (focused on yourself). An example of each has been done for you.

Characteristic:	Loving, Focused on Others:	Unloving, Focused on Myself:
Suffers Long		Impatient, wanting others to do it my way
Is Kind	Speak gently, try to help	
Does Not Envy		
Does Not Parade and Boast		
Does Not Behave Rudely		
Does Not Seek Its Own		
Is Not Easily Provoked		

INQUIRY-ACTION 1.2 (CONTINUED)

Thinks No Evil		
Does Not Rejoice in Iniquity		
Rejoices in Truth		
Bears All Things		
Believes All Things		
Hopes All Things		
Endures All Things		
Never Fails		

INQUIRY-ACTION 1.3

DEMONSTRATING CHRIST-LIKE LOVE— A PERSONAL PLAN OF ACTION

The Basis:

According to John 13:34–35 and 1 John 4:11–12, why should I develop a personal plan of action?

The Question:

If Christ-like love were true in my life, how would it make a difference in my relationships with my parents and friends?

The Plan:

What are specific actions that I need to take to demonstrate Christ-like love?

The Challenge:

Which of these decisions will be the hardest to put into action? Why? How will I overcome the obstacles?

INQUIRY-ACTION 1.4

1 Corinthians 13:4-8a

Vs. 4   **Love**   _____ _____

        and is   _____ ;

    love does   _____ _____ ;

    love does   _____ _____ _____ ,

        is   _____ _____ _____ ;

Vs. 5   **does**   _____ _____ _____ ,

      does   _____ _____ _____ ,

        is   _____ _____ _____ ,

    thinks   _____ _____ ;

Vs. 6   **does**   _____ _____ _____ _____ ,

      but   _____ _____ _____ ;

Vs. 7   _____ _____ _____ ,

    _____ _____ _____ ,

    _____ _____ _____ ,

    _____ _____ _____ .

Vs. 8a   **LOVE** _____ _____ .

WISDOM

Knowledge Used for God's Glory

How many tests do you think you have taken since you have started school? Let's say that you have taken at least two tests each week of the school year. Since a school year is typically 36 weeks long, that means that you have probably taken at least 72 tests in each year that you have been in school. If you have completed six years of school, you have taken at least 432 tests!

You probably do not remember how well you did on each of those tests. But you probably do remember many times that you didn't know the answers to some of the questions. Maybe during those times you said something like this: "I sure wish that I had more wisdom!"

Would it surprise you to know that more wisdom would probably not have helped you to do better on the test? It was knowledge that you needed, not wisdom. Wisdom and knowledge are words that are often confused.

It is quite possible to be very smart but not very wise. "Knowledge" refers to learning facts or information. On the other hand, "wisdom" refers to the practical application of knowledge in order to live a happy and successful life. For the Christian, living a happy and successful life means living according to God's standards. That is why Solomon, the author of Proverbs said, "The fear of the Lord is the beginning of wisdom" (9:10).

Jesus described the difference between the wise man and the foolish man in Matthew 7:24–27. One built his house on the rock, the other on the sand. When the storm came, the foolish man's house collapsed, but the wise man's house, built upon the rock, stood firm. The wise man was the one who, Jesus said, "hears these words of mine and puts them into practice."

Head knowledge is good for tests and quizzes. Good grades will help you achieve your goals in the future. But when the Bible talks about wisdom, it means more than getting good grades or scoring high on an IQ test. God wants you to know how to apply His truth in your life. In order to help us gain wisdom, He gave us the book of Proverbs. There are 915 proverbs, or "wise sayings," contained in the book. If you want true wisdom, the book of Proverbs is the place to start.

Think about the valuable lessons you have learned from your parents, grandparents, teachers and pastor. If you could pick just one lesson you learned, to pass on to your children or grandchildren, what lesson would you choose?

When Solomon was your age, he was living in the palace with his father King David. Solomon's childhood could not be described as very peaceful. Israel was constantly at war with the surrounding nations. There was also immorality and rebellion taking place within the palace walls.

Do you suppose that Solomon might have been thinking about these things when he wrote these proverbs to his son? Solomon knew that the pathway to sin and destruction was a slippery one. He knew how easy it is to be attracted to the things of this world. The most important lesson that Solomon believed he could pass to his son was: To avoid the slippery path, don't watch your feet; watch your heart—for that is where sin's temptation begins (based on Proverbs 6:20–23).

Although Solomon was a very smart man, he has become famous for his wisdom. He learned early in his life that there were two ways to do things—the world's way and God's way. If he wanted to be wise, he had to choose God's way. As you read through the book of Proverbs, note how Solomon is constantly contrasting the world's way and God's way.

Solomon defined wisdom in a single sentence: "The fear of the Lord is the beginning of wisdom" (Proverbs 9:10). By learning to love and respect God above everything else, you will obtain the wisdom that only God can give. Becoming wise is not something that will happen overnight, by the end of the semester, or even by the time you graduate from school. You will continually increase in wisdom as you seek to live according to the principles of God's Word.

Think about the many opportunities that you have every day to respond according to the way of the world or according to God's way. When you are angry with your parents or a friend, how do you respond? Proverbs 14 gives you specific principles on how to handle your anger in a godly way. How would you describe your speech? Do you use profanity? Do you gossip? Do you criticize others? Proverbs 15 has some specific advice in each of these areas.

Are you struggling with sinful thoughts? If the Lord could look into your mind right now, would He be pleased with your thoughts and motives? In Proverbs 16, God shows you how to gain control over your thought life.

Once there was a famous piano player who was loved and respected by people all around the world. One day he overheard a conversation in which he was described as a "genius." He quickly responded, "Genius? For the past 40 years I have practiced at least six hours a day, every day of the week. I am the best in the world because I have worked at it almost every day of my life!"

Certainly this piano player had talent, but he had become the world's greatest pianist because he had spent his entire life putting his talent and knowledge into practice. The same is true with sports. An athlete knows that to be really good, you must practice, practice, practice.

This is the same pattern that you must follow in your life if you want true wisdom. You have already learned many principles from God's Word. Begin right now to practice those Biblical principles that you already know. As you apply God's Word in your life, you will grow in wisdom because you are using knowledge for God's glory.

INQUIRY-ACTION 2.1

WISE SAYINGS FROM PROVERBS

DAY	CHAPTER AND VERSE	SAYING
Monday		A wise person will . . .
Tuesday		A wise person will . . .
Wednesday		A wise person will . . .
Thursday		A wise person will . . .
Friday		A wise person will . . .

INQUIRY-ACTION 2.2

WHAT IS WISDOM?

1. Where does wisdom ultimately come from?

_____

_____

2. Wisdom is not . . . .

_____

_____

3. Wisdom is . . . .

_____

_____

4. What Bible book is good to study if you want to grow in wisdom?

_____

_____

5. Who can get wisdom?

_____

_____

6. Is wisdom easy to develop?

_____

_____

7. Why should a person try to get wisdom?

_____

_____

INQUIRY-ACTION 2.3

WISDOM CHECK

Yes- - - - - - - -No

1. I often act without stopping to think.   5 4 3 2 1 0

2. My friends think I like to take dares and risks.   5 4 3 2 1 0

3. I spend a lot of time just goofing off.   5 4 3 2 1 0

4. It's hard for me to listen to advice from adults.   5 4 3 2 1 0

5. I quickly make up my mind about what I want to do.   5 4 3 2 1 0

6. I depend on my friends a lot for advice.   5 4 3 2 1 0

7. I like to try new things even if they are a little dangerous.   5 4 3 2 1 0

8. I can't wait until I'm old enough to have my own car.   5 4 3 2 1 0

9. I like to go along with my friends even if it means I
    could get into trouble.   5 4 3 2 1 0

10. I give in easily when the group wants to do something.   5 4 3 2 1 0

11. It's hard for me to say "No!" to a friend.   5 4 3 2 1 0

12. I think I'm faced with a lot more temptation than
     others my age.   5 4 3 2 1 0

13. I usually don't think about the consequences of
     something before I do it.   5 4 3 2 1 0

14. Admiration from my friends would generally
     be more important to me than possible punishment.   5 4 3 2 1 0

15. If I've made a wrong choice, it is difficult for me to
     back out and admit my wrong.   5 4 3 2 1 0

INQUIRY-ACTION 2.4

JESUS GROWS IN WISDOM   LUKE 2:40-52

Assume that you are a reporter for "Kids in the News," a local newspaper special section. You have gotten wind of a boy lost from his parents who has been in the Temple for three days astounding the elders with His wisdom. Your editor immediately asks you to write the story, directing you to get the scoop, including the background and reactions of those around him. Write your story below.

INQUIRY-ACTION 2.5

WISE SAYINGS FROM THE BOOK OF PROVERBS

_____1. For the Lord gives wisdom;

A. Therefore get wisdom; and in all your getting, get understanding (4:7).

_____2. My son, do not forget my law,

B. and lean not on your own understanding (3:5).

_____3. Wisdom is the principal thing;

C. but the mouth of the foolish is near destruction (10:14).

_____4. The fear of the Lord is the beginning of knowledge [wisdom];

D. and he who has it will abide in satisfaction; he will not be visited with evil (19:23).

_____5. Commit your works to the Lord,

E. and the knowledge of the Holy One is understanding (9:10).

_____6. The fear of the Lord leads to life;

F. and all the things one may desire cannot be compared with her (8:11).

_____7. He who has a slack hand becomes poor,

G. but fools despise wisdom and instruction (1:7).

_____8. Listen to counsel and receive instruction,

H. but shame shall be the legacy of fools (3:35).

_____9. Trust in the Lord with all your heart,

I. From His mouth comes knowledge and understanding (2:6).

INQUIRY–ACTION 2.5 (CONTINUED)

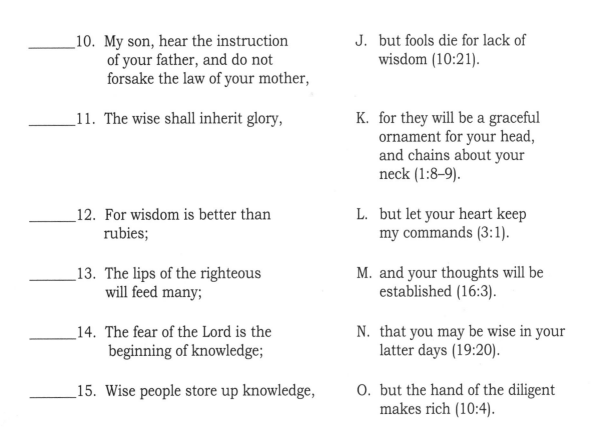

_____10. My son, hear the instruction of your father, and do not forsake the law of your mother,

J.   but fools die for lack of wisdom (10:21).

_____11. The wise shall inherit glory,

K.   for they will be a graceful ornament for your head, and chains about your neck (1:8–9).

_____12. For wisdom is better than rubies;

L.   but let your heart keep my commands (3:1).

_____13. The lips of the righteous will feed many;

M.   and your thoughts will be established (16:3).

_____14. The fear of the Lord is the beginning of knowledge;

N.   that you may be wise in your latter days (19:20).

_____15. Wise people store up knowledge,

O.   but the hand of the diligent makes rich (10:4).

JAMES 3:17–18; 1:5

"But the wisdom that is from above is first pure, then peaceable, gentle, willing to yield, full of mercy and good fruits, without partiality and without hypocrisy. Now the fruit of righteousness is sown in peace by those who make peace. If any of you lacks wisdom, let him ask of God, who gives to all liberally and without reproach, and it will be given to him."

OBEDIENCE

Always Doing What God Says

Every game has rules that must be followed, or else the contestants will be disqualified. The 1980 winner of the Boston Marathon was Rosie Ruiz. She set a women's record of 2:31:56. However, she was stripped of her title because she was accused of jumping out of the crowd and running only the end of the race. Although she claimed that she really did run the race, witnesses testified that she had taken a short cut to get ahead of the rest of the runners. She ran, but not according to the rules, so she failed to win the prize. The Bible says, "And also if anyone competes in athletics, he is not crowned unless he competes according to the rules" (2 Timothy 2:5).

The Apostle Paul used a number of illustrations from sports to describe the Christian life. In 1 Corinthians 9:24–25 he said, "Do you not know that those who run in a race all run, but one receives the prize? Run in such a way that you may obtain it. And everyone who competes for the prize is temperate in all things. Now they do it to obtain a perishable crown, but we for an imperishable crown."

Once again the Apostle Paul used an illustration from track. Paul was not referring to the Boston Marathon, but to the Isthmian Games which were started by Alexander the Great and held every third year in Corinth, Greece. If you traveled to the city of Corinth today, you would still be able to see some of the race's starting blocks in the stone streets.

In order to compete in these Isthmian Games, athletes had to take an oath saying they had trained for at least 10 months. These games were not just for "casual" athletes. They were serious business! By using this illustration, Paul made it very clear that the Christian walk is also serious business. It takes obedience and hard work to be successful in the Christian life.

Obedience begins by recognizing who has legitimate authority in our lives. One day Jesus met a Roman Centurion whose servant was seriously ill (Matthew 8:5–13). Although the Centurion was an important man, he did not feel he was worthy to meet Jesus personally. So he sent a message to Jesus asking for His help. He had no doubt that, if Jesus would come, his servant would be healed. He said, "For I also am a man under authority, having soldiers under me. And I say to this one, 'Go,' and he goes; and to another, 'Come,' and he comes; and to my servant, 'Do this,' and he does it" (Matthew 8:9).

The Centurion understood what it meant to be obedient to those in authority over him. He understood the authority of Jesus and believed that if Jesus told the illness to "Go," it would go!

Jesus was greatly impressed by the response of the Centurion. He said He had not seen such great faith in all of Israel—and this man was a Roman!

Just like the Centurion, we must realize that God is the ultimate authority in our lives. There are two important principles about obedience that every Christian should clearly understand. There is the principle of "delegation" and the principle of "immediate response."

The obedience principle of "delegation" means that God, as the Ultimate Authority, has granted authority to certain individuals. For example, the Bible teaches that parents have authority over children, that we are under the authority of government, that workers are to be obedient to masters, and that we should be under the authority of the spiritual leaders in our local church. Since God has delegated authority to these people, we are to obey them because they have been appointed by God. (Read Romans 13:1–5.)

Have you ever disobeyed your parents? Have you ever seen Christians disobey the laws of their government or fail to follow the spiritual leadership of their pastor or elders? When we fail to obey those authorities that God has placed in our lives, we are directly disobeying Him.

When God speaks, He expects action—not "maybe," not "later," not "I'll think about it," but "yes" and "now." This is the obedience principle known as "immediate response."

Procrastination (putting off until later what we are supposed to do now) is a serious problem. When most people are asked to do something, they usually don't come right out and say "no." It's usually, "How about tomorrow?" or "I'm busy right now, but I'll get to it as soon as I can." These are the types of responses that students often make to parents, teachers or friends.

Have you ever responded to God by saying, "I'll take time to pray tomorrow," or "I'll witness to the new boy in class this weekend"? God expects an immediate response to His request. Remember, partial obedience is disobedience, and delayed obedience is disobedience.

Rosie Ruiz ran part of the race, even the last part. But since she didn't run the whole marathon, she lost.

Your brother can drive the speed limit regularly, but if he speeds past the radar gun, the rest of his obedience doesn't matter. He still gets a ticket.

Most people misunderstand the full meaning of obedience. They feel they are doing well if they just make the effort. For example, instead of swearing all the time, some people think it is "OK" if just a few curse words slip out now and then. Or, instead of outright lying, we think it's fine if we only exaggerate a little.

Replacing one sin with another is not what Jesus had in mind when He said, "If you love me, keep my commandments" (John 14:15). If our love for Jesus is genuine, our total obedience to Him will follow.

Suppose you were asked to write down all of the principles in the Bible in which God has instructed us how to act as a Christian. Of course, the first principles you would probably list would be the Ten Commandments. Then you would probably include such principles as praying daily, witnessing, living a pure life, etc.

If you were to do this exercise, how long would your list be? Would it only be a page in length, or would it take many pages to write down all of the Biblical principles you know?

Once your list was finished, suppose you were asked to underline all of the Biblical principles that you knew you were now obeying. How many of the principles on your list could you underline? The question is really quite simple: "How much of the Word of God do you know that you are not obeying?"

Obedience, whether to God or any authority He has placed over us, is not an option. Remember, obedience is always doing what God says. God's blessing will come to those who obey immediately and completely.

INQUIRY-ACTION 3.1

JOURNAL OF OBEDIENCE

Area of Specific Behavior:	To Whom:	Evaluation:	
		1.	
	What Attitude:	2.	
		3.	
		4.	
		5.	
Area:	To Whom:	Evaluation:	
		1.	
	What Attitude:	2.	
		3.	
		4.	
		5.	
Area:	To Whom:	Evaluation:	
		1.	
	What Attitude:	2.	
		3.	
		4.	
		5.	

INQUIRY-ACTION 3.2

Learning to obey is good for me because

_____

_____

_____

_____

_____

_____

_____

_____

_____

_____

_____

_____

_____

_____

_____

_____

_____

_____

Inquiry-Action 3.3

Obedience Flow Chart

Biblical Relationship ⟶	Example(s) ⟶	Personal Benefit
Obedience to God (Acts 5:29)		
Obedience to parents (Ephesians 6:1)		
Obedience to rulers (Romans 13:1)		
Obedience to spiritual leaders (Hebrews 13:17)		

INQUIRY-ACTION 3.4

HEBREWS 13:16–17

COURAGE

Unafraid to Follow God

Do you know what a fable is? A fable is a fictional story that teaches an important, practical truth. Usually the characters in the story are animals who speak and act like humans.

For centuries fables have been used to teach young students important principles through storytelling. One of the most famous of all storytellers was a man named Aesop. One of his most popular fables is about courage and is entitled, "The Mice in Council."

> Once upon a time all the mice met together in council and discussed the best means of protecting themselves against the attacks of the cat. After several suggestions had been debated, a mouse who was well known and very experienced said, "I think I have a plan which ensures our safety in the future, provided you approve and carry it out. I believe that we should attach a bell around the neck of our enemy the cat, which will by its tinkling warn us of her approach.
>
> This proposal was warmly applauded, and the mice had already decided to adopt it, when another old mouse finally got up on his feet and said, "I agree with you all that the plan before us is an admirable one; but I ask, who is going to put the bell on the cat?"

The lesson found in Aesop's fable is obvious: "TALK IS CHEAP—ACTION REQUIRES COURAGE." Courage has many different names: bravery, fearlessness, nerve, guts and heroism. But whatever it is called, you always know when you are in the presence of someone who has courage.

Gideon is often considered one of the most courageous warriors in the Old Testament. With an army of only 300 men, God gave him complete victory over the armies of the Midianites.

But if you study the life of Gideon before he went into battle, you might question whether or not he was really courageous. In Judges 6:1–10, we learn that the Midianites had been oppressing Israel for seven years. Each year during these seven years, Israel would grow their crops to feed themselves and their cattle. When the time of harvest came, the Midianites would show up and take all of their grain. After seven years of this oppression, the nation of Israel cried out to God for help. We are introduced to Gideon in verse 11. Gideon was hidden in a winepress threshing grain out of sight of the Midianites.

To thresh grain you need a large, flat, open space where you can pile the grain, beat it and throw it into the air so that the wind can blow away the chaff and leave the grain. For a winepress, you need a small space where you can pile the grapes, press them and collect the juice that runs out. In other words, a winepress is no place to be threshing grain. The reason Gideon was threshing grain in the winepress was because he was afraid of the Midianites and did not want to be seen out in the open.

While Gideon was doing his work, the angel of the Lord visited him and said, "The Lord is with you, mighty warrior."

If there was ever anybody who did not feel—or look—like a mighty warrior, it was Gideon! Here he was, threshing grain inside a small winepress so the Midianites could not find him. In verse 13 Gideon responded to the angel of the Lord by saying, "If the Lord is with us, why has all this happened?"

The angel of the Lord did not respond to Gideon. Instead, Gideon was told that God was with him, and that He would deliver Israel from the Midianites. Of course Gideon still had his doubts and fears, but he obeyed. As a result of his courage and obedience, God used him to defeat the mighty army of Midian.

Gideon's story teaches us an important lesson about courage. Courage is not the absence of fear. Fear is a natural emotion that God has given us to protect us from harm. If you are standing on a railroad track and a train is coming, it is a good thing to be scared. Your fear will warn you to get off the track and get out of the way. You are certainly no match for an oncoming train! This is a natural fear that helps protect you from a dangerous situation.

Courage means having fear because you are aware of the dangers, but you go ahead anyway because of the importance of what must be done. A person with courage has the inner strength to "keep on keeping on." In spite of the odds or the difficult problems, a courageous person is determined to be victorious.

David had courage when he picked up a sling, placed a rock in it and killed Goliath. Daniel demonstrated courage when he refused to worship Nebuchadnezzar's statue in Babylon. Elijah showed courage when he stood up to the prophets of Baal on top of Mount Carmel. Moses was courageous when he told Pharaoh to let God's people go.

The fact is: It is impossible to live victoriously for Christ without courage. God's ways are not the ways of the world. Because Christians are children of God, they will be called upon to stand up for what is right. This will take courage. God's challenge to Joshua (Joshua 1:6–7, 9) is just as important to us today: "Be strong and courageous!"

Remember, real courage is not found just on the battlefield or by accomplishing some brave act. The real tests of courage are inner tests. When you are all alone and you have the opportunity to take something that does not belong to you, what do you do? When your friends choose to do something that you know does not please the Lord, to whom are you faithful?

These are the inner tests of courage that you will face every day of your life. If you successfully pass these tests, you will be ready to serve the Lord when greater opportunities come.

Are you courageous? Honestly now—are you? Are you quick to quit? Do you run away from situations when they get too difficult? With others who are choosing to do wrong, do you do right?

Only you can answer these questions. The Lord is looking for men and women who are courageous. You can take that first courageous step, right now, by praying, "Lord, from this day on I will choose to do what's right, no matter how difficult it may be."

Inquiry-Action 4.1

Study on Courage

Box 1: The focus of this week's study is _____.

Box 2: Synonyms

Box 3: Antonyms

Box 4: Circumstances Which Reveal Courage:

INQUIRY-ACTION 4.1 (CONTINUED)

STUDY ON COURAGE

Box 5: Definition:

Box 6: Bible Illustrations

Person	Situation	Scripture
1.		
2.		
3.		

Box 7: The Lesson for Me:

INQUIRY-ACTION 4.2

TEST OF COURAGE

1. **Character Trait: Courage means:**

   _____

2. **What I learned about this trait:**

   _____

   _____

   _____

3. **The test of courage that is most difficult for me is:**

   _____

   _____

   _____

4. **What I need to do to overcome this challenge (and others) is:**

   _____

   _____

   _____

INQUIRY-ACTION 4.3

JOSHUA 1:9—WORD SEARCH

Use your Bible, or your memory, to locate all the words in the giant word-find.
Copy the verse at the bottom.

```
O W G Y M O D A G R D E T E Z C Y K H
T P S S R T F O W I O Y M A B Y H T L
W I L L H B E J S A G B D U N A H I C
V W W O T S J M F Z R E J T O U O O A
M R U P T M A R C F O U W F M T M D C
R S R B A Y A Z O J Y R N B Q M D W A
N U E M E I U E Z U O B L T A O W D S
P O F D D R H X W X J E G N O H E Y W
A E T K G A E Y W F A G D G C G F O X
C G E N V E O V B H S E L L A Z N O F
T A S R B F E I E K D G M R L E U A R
R R Y O U B N E T R I U U X I I Z U R
S U H A V E D H H A E O Q T L W Y O F
I O Y H C F D T X T C H H W Y G N D J
R C F T N R A V H S U E W B T Z T N O
U K G S O J L T I E R M D G N O R T S
O T O L T U I D O M G B K F E V B M V
Y B D B K W D E I F I R R E T H V L D
O A N D E Y R E V E O S R E H T I H W
```

ATTENTIVENESS

The First Step to Success

In the early days of this century, a steamship company advertised for a telegraph operator. On the day the interviews were to be given, so many people showed up that the company's waiting room was packed. Every seat was taken and a number of people were forced to stand. Although the room was filled with strangers, they soon got to know each other and talked about their hopes of getting the job as a telegraph operator. As the hour for interviewing came and passed, no one from the company appeared. As the afternoon grew later and later, the applicants became more and more restless.

Suddenly one of the men in the room jumped to his feet, opened the door to the inner office and disappeared inside. Everyone else in the waiting room wondered what was wrong with the man. Time continued to pass, and the applicants became more restless.

Finally, a company official opened the door. "Thank you all for coming today," he said. "The position has been filled."

Everyone in the office was shocked and began to angrily accuse the company officials of unfair treatment. The company official responded, "From the time interviews were set to begin, we have been broadcasting in Morse code over our intercom the instructions to come into the inner office and ask for Mr. Avery. This gentleman here was the only one who heard the instructions. Because he was paying attention, he has earned the job."

How many times have you done something incorrectly or gotten into trouble because you had failed to pay attention? These men lost the opportunity for a job they really wanted because they were too interested in listening to each other and not paying attention to what was going on around them.

Our failure to pay attention not only causes problems in our lives, but also robs us of the opportunity of helping others. Attentiveness is shown through our words and our actions.

James said, "So then, my beloved brethren, let every man be swift to hear, slow to speak, slow to wrath " (James 1:19). The way in which James has instructed us to use words is exactly the opposite of what most people do. Wouldn't you agree that many people get angry first, then say some things they shouldn't, and finally listen to what really happened?

One day Julie came home from her eighth-grade class meeting very upset. "Mrs. Jackson is so unfair," she said to her Mom. "She is the worst class sponsor we have ever had."

"What happened?" her mother asked.

"We have to change the date of our eighth-grade class trip. It's going to mean so much more work for the class officers," Julie replied.

"I think she said something about a conflict, but I can't remember," Julie explained.

"Did she say she would help the officers with the extra work?" Julie's mother asked.

"I'm not sure," Julie said. "It seems she said something about helping us, but I can't remember."

Julie's mother then suggested that she go back to Mrs. Jackson and apologize.

"APOLOGIZE! For what? What did I do?"

"You didn't listen, Julie," her mother said. "You obviously became so upset because of the date change, you didn't hear another word she said."

Listening carefully to the words of others is one of the most important lessons you can learn. It is the first step to success in relationships with others, in school and in everything you do in the future.

We should not only be attentive to the words of others, but to the needs of others as well. Do you remember the story from the book of Job? Job had lost his family, his possessions, and then became afflicted with sores all over his body. In a terrible situation like this, you would think his friends would have come to him with comforting words. But this was not so. Job complained that his three friends tormented and crushed him with their words (Job 19:2). In a time of personal hardship, Job's friends were not paying attention to his needs.

Ask yourself if there are students in your class who have needs. For example, are there students who would like to have a friend but have no friends? Do you know of students who are having trouble in their classes or not getting along with their parents? All around you there are people with needs. Are you concerned about their needs? Are you willing to reach out and help them rather than criticizing or ignoring them?

Let's not forget the most important type of listening we need to practice: listening to God. God is constantly speaking to us. He speaks to us through His Word, through prayer, and through the counsel of others. But often we are like those who were applying for the telegraph operator's job at that steamship company. We are so busy talking to each other we don't hear what God is saying to us.

As king, David had many important responsibilities. On top of that, people came to him every day for advice to solve their problems. From the moment he got up in the morning until he went to bed in the evening, David was busy conducting business for the people of Israel.

Yet in spite of all his responsibilities and his busy schedule, he knew the importance of spending time listening to God. In Psalm 46, David reminds us of the strength and help that God provides every day. Verse 10 says, "Be still and know that I am God."

Those are good words of advice to each of us. Find a place and a time that you can get alone with God and listen to what He has to say to you. Begin today to learn how to pay better attention to God and to others. Learn to listen with both your ears and your heart! Attentiveness is your first step to success with God and in your relationships with others.

INQUIRY-ACTION 5.1

BE ATTENTIVE!

Exodus 15:26

1 Samuel 3:10

Nehemiah 1:6
Nehemiah 8:3

Job 37:2

Psalm 4:3
Psalm 17:1
Psalm 55:2
Psalm 81:13
Psalm 85:8
Psalm 86:6
Psalm 130:2
Psalm 141:8

Proverbs 1:8
Proverbs 4:20
Proverbs 8:33
Proverbs 15:3
Proverbs 19:20
Proverbs 22:17

Ecclestiastes 5:1

Isaiah 21:7
Isaiah 28:14

Jeremiah 29:12

Ezekiel 40:4

Matthew 11:15
Matthew 15:10
Matthew 18:17
Matthew 24:42
Matthew 25:13
Matthew 26:38
Matthew 26:41

Mark 4:20
Mark 4:24
Mark 9:7
Mark 13:33
Mark 13:35
Mark 13:37

Luke 2:8
Luke 8:18
Luke 9:35
Luke 11:28
Luke 19:48

John 5:25
John 10:27

Acts 4:19
Acts 9:4
Acts 10:33
Acts 22:26
Acts 26:3

1 Corinthians 8:9

1 Thessalonians 5:6

1 Timothy 6:20

2 Timothy 4:5

Hebrews 2:1–3
Hebrews 3:7, 15

2 Peter 1:19

Revelation 3:20
Revelation 13:9

INQUIRY-ACTION 5.2

INFORMATION PROCESSING

1. We take in all kinds of general information—more than _____ pieces at any given time.

2. Although we can do many, many _____ (without conscious thinking) tasks at the same time, we can only do one

   _____ (focused attention) task at a time.

3. Even when we pay attention, only a few pieces of information (up to 7 or 8) can be held in _____-_____

   _____ .

4. To mentally process information means to _____ it to other pieces of information we know. In other words, we label, categorize, contrast, analyze and fit together _____ information with

   _____ information.

5. To keep the information in our memories, we must do several things:

   1) _____

   2) _____

   3) _____

   4) _____

These things are why attentiveness is the first step to success. Without it we can never learn anything and, consequently, never do anything successfully.

Inquiry-Action 5.3

Personal Time Analysis

There are 168 hours in a week. You are awake approximately 100 hours each week. How many hours do you spend each week personally interacting with the following?

____ Relatives
   brothers___
   sisters___
   parents___
   other family members___

____ School/Job
   teachers___
   others (principals,
     librarians, monitors)___
   employer___

____ Friends
   at school___
   at church___

____ Media
   television___
   video games___
   tapes/CDs___
   movies___
   newspapers___
   magazines___
   books___

How many hours do you spend each week listening to God?

____ Prayer
____ Bible study
____ Sunday school/church
____ memorizing Scripture

____ reading Christian
     literature
____ listening to Christian
     music

INQUIRY-ACTION 5.4

PROVERBS 4:20–21

Use a marker to write the verses as they appear in your Bible. Use the page as a study guide.

_____   _____ (Who?)

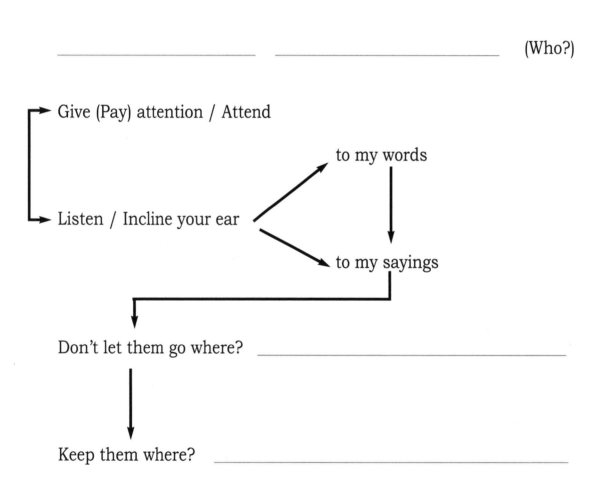

Give (Pay) attention / Attend

to my words

Listen / Incline your ear

to my sayings

Don't let them go where?   _____

Keep them where?   _____

FAITH

Acting on God's Promises

Faith—it's one of those concepts like "justice" or "truth" that you may vaguely understand but would probably find hard to define or explain to others.

The dictionary says that faith is "belief not based on proof or evidence." But is that what Biblical faith really means? The writer of Hebrews says, "Now faith is the substance of things hoped for, the evidence of things not seen" (11:1). For the Christian, faith is believing in what God has said in His Word and acting accordingly.

What you believe about God is the most important thing about you. It will determine how you live and the choices you will make. Do you believe God will save you? Do you believe that God is able to take care of you? Do you believe that God hears you when you pray?

Faith is our response to God's power and trustworthiness. Yet before we grow in faith, we must first have faith in Him as our personal Savior and Lord. There are two types of faith: "saving faith" and "walking faith." The study of astronaut James Irwin clearly illustrates the difference between these two types of faith.

Irwin was born in Pittsburgh and became a Christian when he was eleven. He said that although he accepted the Lord as a boy, he did not walk with the Lord as he should have. His interests were not really in spiritual things.

After attending high school, Irwin received an appointment to the U.S. Naval Academy. He decided to go into the Air Force and enter flight training. All it took was one trip in a P-51 fighter plane and he was hooked. From that time on, all he wanted to do was fly; the faster the plane, the better.

In May 1966, he was chosen for the Apollo program. The goal of the Apollo program was to put men on the moon. That is what Irwin had always dreamed of. He now was given the opportunity to fly faster and farther than anyone had ever done before. While all he could think about was the actual flight to the moon, he completely overlooked how high his spiritual flight might be.

It was as the astronauts began their journey to the moon that Irwin became most aware of God's presence. "As we flew into space, we had a new sense of ourselves, of the earth and of the nearness of God. I sensed the beginning of some sort of change taking place in me."

After the flight, Irwin began speaking publicly about what God had taught him during those days in space. As the message spread, many requests came for him to speak elsewhere. In 1972 he retired from NASA in order to devote all his time to sharing the message of Jesus Christ. He wanted to tell others about how faith in Jesus Christ will save them from their sins. But he also wanted to tell them about the faith that comes in walking with God day by day. The same God Who walked with him on the moon walks with us each and every day of our lives.

The story of James Irwin illustrates the ideas of both saving faith and walking faith. First, a person must come to Christ asking forgiveness for sins and trusting Him as personal Savior (Romans 10:9–10). This is saving faith. From that time on, a person cooperates with the Holy Spirit to become like Christ—to be and to do as God wants (Philippians 2:12). That is walking faith.

When was the last time you took a walk just for the enjoyment of going for a walk? Going for a walk is a pretty safe activity, unless you are careless about where you are going.

Walking through a busy city means watching out for traffic, avoiding dark alleys and staying in safe areas. If you're walking through the countryside, you need to be careful not to become lost. It is also possible that you could encounter unexpected, unfriendly animals.

A Christian walking through this world faces spiritual hazards similar to those found in the city and in the country. Because this world is corrupted by sin, Christians must beware of the dangers around them. That's why the Apostle Paul describes the devil as "your adversary . . . (who) walks about like a roaring lion, seeking whom he may devour" (1 Peter 5:8).

But, there is a Companion Who walks with the Christian throughout his life. David describes this companion when he says, "Yea, though I walk through the valley of the shadow of death, I will fear no evil; For You are with me; Your rod and Your staff, they comfort me" (Psalm 23:4). Walking with God is the Christian's key to a safe journey through this life and throughout all eternity.

As you begin your walk of faith, read the letters (epistles) of Peter, John and Jude. These letters were meant as your "travel guides" as you walk with the Lord each day.

Peter's two letters describe the struggles of the disciples as they tried to follow in the footsteps of Jesus. The disciples soon learned that the Christian's walk was not easy. Peter reminds us that even though it may be difficult at times, we must continue to follow in the steps of Jesus. "For to this you were called, because Christ also suffered for us, leaving us an example, that you should follow His steps" (1 Peter 2:21).

While Peter's two letters remind us that Jesus will keep us safe as we walk in faith with Him, the three letters of John describe the characteristics of someone who is walking in faith. They explain how we should "walk in the light," "walk in the truth" and "walk in His commandments."

Jude's short letter is like a red, flashing warning light. He warns against the temptations that will come as you walk by faith with God.

The Christian life begins with saving faith. Have you accepted Christ as your Savior? John 3:16 tells us, "For God so loved the world that He gave His only begotten Son, that whoever believes in Him should not perish but have everlasting life." This is the first step to the Christian life. It is not possible to walk by faith if you have not first been saved by faith. If you have accepted Jesus Christ as your Savior, are you now walking in faith?

Stop for a moment and think about what you do and say on a typical day. Are your actions and words demonstrating that you are walking in faith? Can you think of anything you have done or said in the past few days that would lead others to believe you are not a Christian?

Remember, Christianity is about faith. It begins with faith in Jesus Christ as your Savior. It continues, for the rest of your life, as you walk by faith in obedience to His Word.

Inquiry-Action 6.1

Fundamental Facts on Faith

A. Mark 9:21–24

B. Romans 5:1–2

C. Romans 10:9–10

D. Ephesians 2:8–9

E. Colossians 2:6–7

F. 2 Timothy 4:7–8

G. Hebrews 11:1–2

H. Hebrews 11:6

I. James 2:17, 20

J. 1 Peter 1:8

____ 1. Faith means trusting God and His promises even though we can't always see them.

____ 2. It is impossible to please God without faith.

____ 3. Faith is a gift from God.

____ 4. If we need more faith, we can ask God for it.

____ 5. Saving faith means trusting Christ to forgive our sins and help us live a life pleasing to God.

____ 6. Saving faith gives us peace with God and access to His grace.

____ 7. After salvation we are to grow in our faith.

____ 8. True faith produces faithfulness in our lives. In other words, faith not expressed in works/behavior has no life.

____ 9. The growth of faith gives us great joy.

____ 10. The end of our faith is eternal life.

INQUIRY-ACTION 6.2

DEFINING FAITH

Ask a parent to complete the first section.

A definition of faith is:

Save the remaining part for class discussion.

Reactions:

1.

2.

3.

My definition of Faith:

INQUIRY-ACTION 6.3
SAVING FAITH AND WALKING FAITH

Saving Faith

What It Is:
How I Experienced It:

Walking Faith

What It Is:	
Characteristics When It's Strong:	Characteristics When It's Weak:

The Lesson for Me:

INQUIRY-ACTION 6.4

ROMANS 1:17

Complete the outline using a marker to write out the verse as it appears in your Bible.

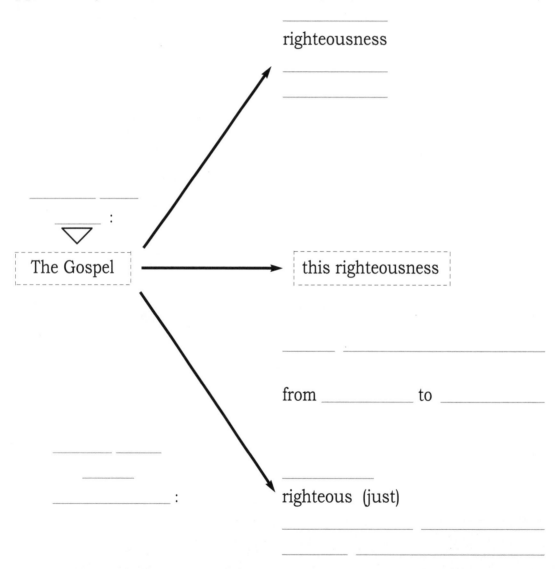

_____
righteousness
_____
_____

_____ _____ :

The Gospel

this righteousness

_____ _____

from _____ to _____

_____ _____

_____ :

_____
righteous (just)

_____ _____
_____ _____

RESPONSIBILITY

Demonstrating Reliable Conduct in Every Situation

Once there were two men who were walking along a forest path late at night. Suddenly, both fell into a large, deep pit. It looked like it would be impossible to escape without some kind of help. One of the men broke into tears and sat in the corner of the hole. All he could do was think about the terrible situation he was in. The other man immediately began to look for a way of escape. As his fingers moved along the sides of the dark pit, his hand touched a long tree root hanging from the side of the wall. He quickly pulled himself out of the pit, then helped his complaining friend out also.

When it comes to taking responsibility, there are two kinds of people in the world. Faced with a challenge or difficult situation, some take responsibility and some don't. In other words, there are those who try to solve the problem and those who become part of the problem.

Let's call this first type of responsibility "opportunity responsibility." When God gives you an opportunity, He expects you to be responsible and take advantage of that opportunity. The parable of the talents (Matthew 25:14–29) illustrates the importance of "opportunity responsibility."

This parable contrasts the difference between those who take advantage of the opportunities given to them and those who don't. The servants who had invested the master's talents and earned additional talents were rewarded. The servant who hid the talent, fearing he would fail, was condemned as wicked and lazy.

The lesson is very clear. When God gives us an opportunity, He expects us to do everything we can to be successful in that opportunity. God is constantly giving us "opportunity responsibilities." There are classmates who need help with their homework, there are those in your school who need a friend and there are those you know who do not know Jesus Christ as their Savior. What have you done to fulfill your "opportunity responsibilities"?

The second type of responsibility is familiar to everyone. It is called "personal responsibility." Every day you are faced with choices: Should you go out with your friends or do your homework? Should you clean up your room or play video games? Making the right choices is one example of showing "personal responsibility."

Have you ever said, "I didn't do it" when you really did? Sometimes we may choose to lie rather than face the consequences of our actions. This is the second type of "personal responsibility." We must honor God by taking responsibility for the consequences of our words as well as our actions.

One of the clearest examples of taking personal responsibility is found in Luke 15:11–32, the parable of the prodigal son. The younger son wanted independence from his father and his family, so he took the inheritance that belonged to him and left home. It was not long before he had lost everything and was reduced to the level of a beggar. He finally returned home, took responsibility for his actions, and asked for forgiveness. His father graciously accepted him back into the family.

God, as well as those in authority over you, expects certain things from you. Responsibility is learning what those things are and then completing what should be done. This is the type of responsibility shown by the missionary Sheldon Jackson.

When you hear the word "reindeer," what do you think about? Does it remind you of Christmas, the North Pole or snow?

For many native Alaskans, the reindeer is the primary source of food, clothing and transportation. Yet if it had not been for the dedicated work of Sheldon Jackson, the reindeer might not be in Alaska today.

It was during his missionary work that Rev. Jackson realized the terrible living conditions of the Alaskans. For many years, hunters had been killing the whales and seals that the Alaskans depended on for food and clothing. The slaughter of these animals had been so great that the Alaskans were nearly to the point of starvation.

Although most people believe that reindeer come from Alaska, that is not true. Reindeer are originally from Lapland and Siberia. It was during his missionary travels that Rev. Jackson first saw these reindeer. He knew immediately that they were the solution to the Alaskan problem.

He went to the U.S. Government to get help to import these reindeer, but no one would provide him with any money. In 1891, he raised about $2,000 from private sources and imported 16 reindeer from Siberia. The following year, he was able to raise enough money to bring in another 141 animals.

Finally, the government agreed to provide money for the project. By the early 1900's, the size of the herd grew to over 1,000. Finding food plentiful, the number of reindeer increased to 500,000 by the mid-1930's. The Alaskans were now assured of a source of food and leather.

Rev. Jackson recognized the opportunity that God had placed before him and accepted the responsibility to do all that he could to be obedient to God's direction. Even though no one would help him at the beginning, he did not quit. Nothing was going to stop him from doing what he knew he must do. Rev. Jackson clearly understood the importance of "opportunity responsibility."

Long before God gave him this opportunity, Sheldon Jackson had shown "personal responsibility." For nearly 40 years, he had served God throughout the world. It began when he accepted the Lord as his Savior at the age of eight. From that moment on, he accepted the responsibility to prepare himself for God's ministry. He knew that before God could give him responsibilities of service, he had to first be responsible for his personal life.

God desires to entrust each of us with opportunities to serve Him. But first we must demonstrate that we are responsible individuals.

How have you shown responsible behavior before God? Do you accept your responsibilities at home? What is the responsible way for you to behave at school? With your friends?

Only you are responsible for what you say and what you do. Are you willing to accept this type of personal responsibility? If so, God will bless you and use you in ways you could only dream about.

Inquiry-Action 7.1

Characteristics of Responsibility

Responsibility is demonstrated in many ways. The Bible describes a number of ways that responsibility should be shown in a believer's life. Match the Scripture portion on the right with a characteristic of responsibility listed in the left column.

_____ **Cautiousness**   (careful)

_____ **Decisiveness**   (determined)

_____ **Diligence**   (earnest)

_____ **Initiative**   (first step)

_____ **Neatness**   (clean and tidy)

_____ **Punctuality**   (on time)

_____ **Resourcefulness**   (clever and capable)

_____ **Thoroughness**   (exact; painstaking)

_____ **Thriftiness**   (saving wisely)

A. Proverbs 18:15

B. Ecclesiastes 3:1

C. 1 Corinthians 14:40

D. Colossians 3:23

E. Deuteronomy 4:9

F. James 1:5

G. Romans 12:21

H. Luke 16:10

I. Luke 16:11

INQUIRY-ACTION 7.2

THE STORY OF THE TALENTS

The Setting: Once upon a time, a father had three teenage sons who had varying degrees of ability on which he based their allowances. To one he gave $50, to another $20, and to the third $10. After a couple of weeks, he asked them to account for the money.

What Happened:

_____

_____

_____

_____

The Lesson:

_____

_____

_____

INQUIRY-ACTION 7.3

RESPONSIBILITY PRINCIPLES

1. _____

_____

2. _____

_____

3. _____

_____

4. _____

_____

5. _____

_____

6. _____

_____

7. _____

_____

INQUIRY-ACTION 7.4

MICAH 6:8

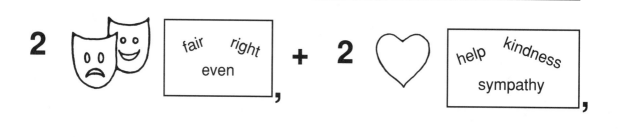

INQUIRY-ACTION 7.5

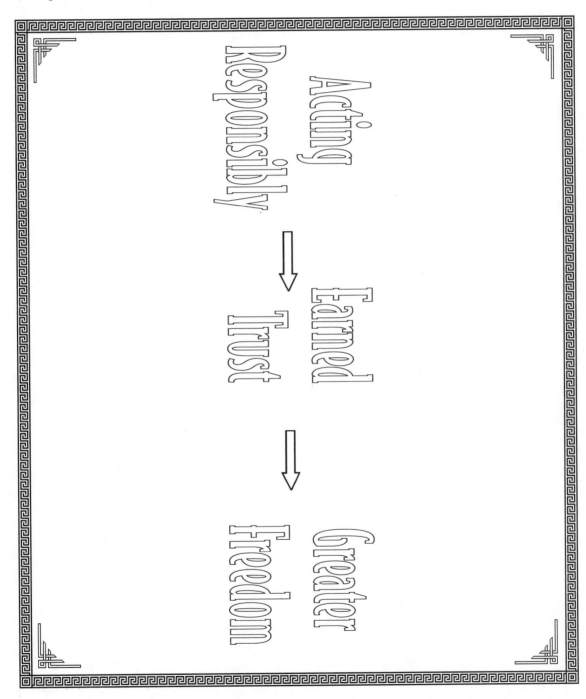

THANKFULNESS

An Attitude of Gratitude to God

Many years ago, a group of travelers toured South America. While visiting Brasilia, the capital of Brazil, they met a number of missionaries involved in translation work among the primitive Indian tribes in South America. By learning the language of these tribes, the missionaries were able to translate the Scriptures into their languages.

During a discussion concerning the difficulties of their work, a young missionary said, "In our tribal group, there is no word for "thank you." Does anyone have any ideas?"

After further discussion, the missionaries all agreed that none of their tribal groups had a word for "thank you." The idea of thankfulness did not exist in their cultures.

What would it be like if you were unable to express your thankfulness to others or have them express theirs to you? Each of us needs encouragement. We should always be looking for every opportunity to express our appreciation to others for what they have done for us. Yet without the proper words, our expression of "thanks" could not be communicated.

Picture an 8-ounce glass with 4 ounces of water. Would you say that the glass is half full or half empty? In other words, are you focusing on the water that is there or the negative fact that there is no water in half of the glass? Often in the situations we face in our own lives, we focus on the negative and forget to thank God for all He has done for us.

The hero of Daniel Defoe's famous novel, *Robinson Crusoe*, knew how to count his blessings in every situation. Crusoe, shipwrecked and a castaway on a deserted island, had every reason to be discouraged and depressed. But he did the smart thing—he sat down, looked his problems squarely in the eye, counted his blessings, and gave thanks to God for His goodness.

In spite of the difficult situation in which he found himself, he was able to find a reason to be thankful. As you read the following lists, notice how Crusoe found a reason to be thankful in the midst of each hardship.

Hardship	Thankfulness
I am cast upon a horrible, desolate island, without any hope of recovery.	But I am alive and not drowned as all my ship's company was.
I am singled out and separated from all the world.	But I am also singled out from all the ship's crew and spared from death. Just as God has saved me from death, He can save me from this condition.
I am divided from mankind, banished from society.	But I am not starving or perishing in a barren place. There is food available to me.
I have no clothes to cover me.	But I am in a hot climate where, if I had clothes, I could hardly wear them.
I am without any defense or means to resist any violence of man or beast.	But I am cast on an island where I see no wild beasts to hurt me as I saw on the

coast of Africa; what if I had
been shipwrecked there?

I have no soul to speak to.

But God wonderfully sent
the ship near enough to
the shore that I have gotten
enough things to meet all
my needs.

Robinson Crusoe knew the importance of thanksgiving. But more than that, he had learned how to turn thanksgiving into "thanks-living." He had learned to apply the message of the Psalmist to his own life: "O give thanks unto the Lord; for he is good: for his mercy endureth forever" (Psalm 136:1). The fictional character Robinson Crusoe had learned what it meant to have an attitude of gratitude to God. Many scholars believe that Defoe's famous character represents Defoe's own attitude of thanksgiving to God.

Too many Christians do not express an attitude of thankfulness on a daily basis. They have become so consumed with their own desires and possessions that they no longer know how to be thankful. If they were shipwrecked on an island, they certainly would not have responded like Robinson Crusoe did.

If you want to practice "thanks-living," start developing the following habits in your life. First, look for the good in everything. This is what Robinson Crusoe did. Even in his difficult situation, he knew that he had to focus on his blessings and not his hardships.

Do you enjoy being around a negative person? Probably not, because that person's negative comments take the joy out of your relationship with that person. As a matter of fact, you know that if you are around a negative person for too long, your attitude will be affected by his attitude; so you avoid that person.

We can look for the good or the bad in any situation. But as you focus your attention on the good, you will experience the joy of "thanks-living."

A second important habit to develop is to give thanks ahead of time for what God is going to do in your life. Do you worry about whether or not you are going to make the team, pass your next science test or make new friends at school? Realize that God knows your concerns and has answered your prayers before you have even asked. Place your future totally in His hands. Thank Him in advance for what He is doing in your life. This habit of "thanks-living" will bring you peace, no matter what you experience throughout the rest of your life.

Finally, and the most difficult of all, give thanks for all of the problems and challenges you face. By facing our challenges and overcoming them, we grow stronger, wiser and more capable of facing future challenges in our lives. God knows all about the struggles you face each day. Thank Him for the opportunity to learn from the problems He has placed before you.

Remember the words of the Psalmist: "Enter into his gates with thanksgiving, and into his courts with praise. Be thankful to Him, and bless His name. For the Lord is good; His mercy is everlasting, and His truth endures to all generations " (Psalm 100:4–5).

Thankfulness is an attitude of gratitude to God. Right now, start practicing thanksgiving in all you do. Each of us has so much to be thankful for. God is honored when we recognize His goodness to us.

INQUIRY-ACTION 8.1

THANKSGIVING

I'm thankful, dear Lord, with all my heart,
For the gifts, through the year, which You did impart;
Thankful I live in the land of the free,
With its peace, vast wealth, and prosperity.

Thankful for graces You've sent, rich and rare,
The fruits, the flowers, the birds in the air;
Thankful I live in this prosperous age
Where science has written a great full page

Of wonderful feats for us to employ
To lessen our labors, increase our joy.
I'm thankful for home with its loving ties,
Where they truly love, care, and sympathize.

—Josephine M. Powers

INQUIRY-ACTION 8.2

BENEFITS OF THANKFULNESS

1. _____

_____

2. _____

_____

3. _____

_____

4. _____

_____

5. _____

_____

6. _____

_____

7. _____

_____

INQUIRY-ACTION 8.3

DEVELOPING A THANKFUL ATTITUDE

1. _____

_____

_____

_____

_____

2. _____

_____

_____

_____

_____

3. _____

_____

_____

_____

**C
O
U
N
T
E
R
S**

1. _____

_____

_____

_____

_____

2. _____

_____

_____

_____

_____

3. _____

_____

_____

_____

INQUIRY-ACTION 8.4

PSALM 136:1-3

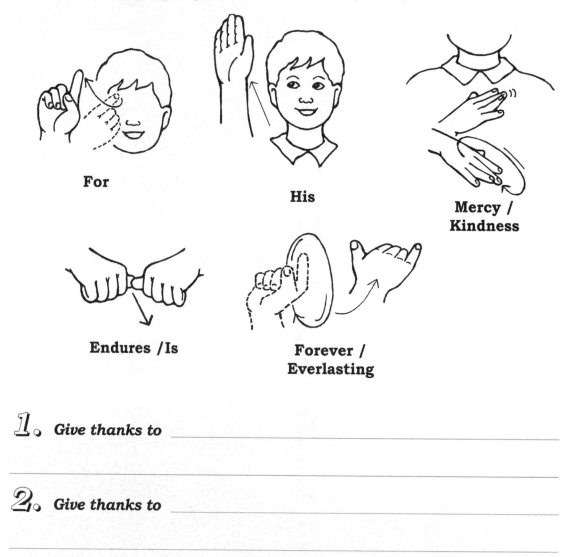

For

His

Mercy /
Kindness

Endures /Is

Forever /
Everlasting

1. **Give thanks to** _____

2. **Give thanks to** _____

3. **Give thanks to** _____

HONESTY

Always the Best Policy

Has your dog ever eaten your homework? Or have you used some other type of excuse to explain why you didn't have your homework ready to turn in when the teacher asked you for it? Think about the last time you were not prepared for class. Did you have an honest reason for not being prepared, or did you lie?

Lying is one of the two types of dishonesty. Lying is not being honest with our words. Do you know what the other type of dishonesty is? It is stealing. Stealing is not being honest in our actions. The Bible has much to say about the importance of honest words and honest actions.

Honesty is so important to God that He addressed two of the Ten Commandments to this subject. In the Eighth Commandment (Exodus 20:15) He said, "You shall not steal." It was in this Commandment that He condemned dishonest actions. In the next Commandment, God condemned lying when He said, "You shall not bear false witness against your neighbor." In these two Commandments, God described clearly that He expects us to act honestly.

The story is told of a young boy who asked his father, "Dad, did you ever cheat?"

His father replied, "Yes. In the fourth grade, I copied the word 'piano' off Janet's paper during a spelling test. I hadn't missed a spelling word all year, and I couldn't stand the thought of losing that gold star on my chart because of one word."

"Then, in the eighth grade, I couldn't remember what the outer ring of the sun was called. When my friend Tom whispered 'corona' to someone else, I convinced myself I would have remembered it eventually and wrote it down."

"Dad," his son asked, "were there any other times?"

His father thought for a moment. He remembered the time he cheated on his golf score and also the times he had cheated on his taxes. As he thought for a few more minutes, a number of other examples of dishonesty flooded his mind. He soon realized that over the years he had developed a pattern of dishonesty that had gone unnoticed.

Dishonesty had become a common response in this father's life. In much the same way, dishonesty has become common throughout today's society. When given the opportunity, individuals think nothing of lying, cheating or stealing. As a matter of fact, many people brag about what they are able to get away with. When a society is no longer bound by the principles of honesty, distrust grows and anarchy soon takes over.

Dishonesty only advances the cause of Satan. In John 8:44, Jesus described Satan in the following way, "He was a murderer from the beginning, and does not stand in the truth, because there is no truth in him. When he speaks a lie, he speaks from his own resources; for he is a liar and the father of it."

Jesus was very clear that Satan is the origin of lies and dishonesty. Jesus also made it very clear that those who ignore the truth are the children of Satan. Certainly, these are strong words. But Jesus wanted us to know that dishonesty is an abomination in His sight.

Remember, people who are dishonest are actually rejecting the Lord Jesus Christ. In John 14:6, Jesus is described as "the way, the truth, and the life." If we call ourselves followers of Jesus Christ, then we must be honest in all things. If dishonesty describes the way we live our lives, then we are followers of Satan, because the truth is not in us. (See 1 John 1:6.)

If honesty has not characterized your life, are you ready to make a change? If so, begin by confessing the sin of dishonesty to Jesus. Then remember the promise of

1 John 1:9, "If we confess our sins, He is faithful and just to forgive us our sins and to cleanse us from all unrighteousness."

After you have confessed your sin, you must begin to develop the habit of honesty in your life. You can establish a reputation for honesty if you will follow these principles:

Principle One: Keep your promises.
If you say you are going to do something, then keep your commitment. Don't promise to do something that you are unable or unwilling to fulfill.

Principle Two: Accept responsibility.
Take the blame when you are to blame. If you are wrong, don't make excuses. Accept full responsibility for your actions.

Principle Three: Acknowledge others.
Don't try to take credit for the accomplishments of others. When others are successful, give them the recognition that they deserve.

If lying or stealing characterize your life, now is the time to put these three principles into action. If you do not follow these principles, eventually your true character will be discovered. Remember, honesty is always the best policy!

INQUIRY-ACTION 9.1

READ LEVITICUS 19:11–13

Negative Command:	Do Not Steal	Do Not Lie	Do Not Cheat/ Defraud/Slander Others
Positive Purpose:			
Consequence of Disobedience:			
Consequence of Obedience:			
The Lesson for Me:			

INQUIRY-ACTION 9.2

THE DEVIL—THE FATHER OF LIES

I. The Names of the Devil

    A. _____ is the personal name of the devil, meaning _____ (1 Chronicles 21:1; Job 1–2).

    B. _____ means _____ or false accuser. This is the common name used in the New Testament.

    C. _____ (1 Thessalonians 3:5)

    D. the _____ one (Matthew 13:19)

    E. the _____ of the power of the _____ (Ephesians 2:2)

    F. the _____ of our brethren (Revelation 12:10)

II. The Influence of the Devil

    A. His titles reflect his _____ of this _____ system.

        1. the _____ of this world (John 12:31)

        2. the _____ of this age (2 Corinthians 4:4)

        3. the _____ of the power of the air (Ephesians 2:2)

    B. He exercises his evil _____ through _____.

        1. i.e., at the time Jesus _____ _____ _____ (Matthew 12:28–29; Acts 10:38)

        2. i.e., at the time of Jesus' _____ _____ (Revelation 9:3–17; 12:12; 18:2)

III. The Power of the Devil

    A. Satan's power is _____. He is subject to God's _____ (Job 1:7–12; Luke 4:6; 2 Thessalonians 2:7–8).

    B. Satan is _____ to _____ God's people (Luke 13:16; Hebrews 2:14), but is never _____ to _____ an ultimate victory over them (John 14:30–31; 16:33).

INQUIRY-ACTION 9.2 (CONTINUED)

    C. Satan's nature is _____. He consistently attempts to oppose
        _____, His _____ and His _____
        (Job 1:7; Matthew 13:24–28; John 8:44).

    D. Satan is always _____ to man's best interests (1 Chronicles
        21:1; Zechariah 3:1–2).

IV. The Character of Satan
    A. _____, presumptuous (1 Timothy 3:6)
    B. _____ (Ephesians 2:2)
    C. _____ (1 John 2:13)
    D. _____ and _____ (1 Peter 5:8)
    E. _____ (John 8:44)
    F. can _____ as an _____ (2 Corinthians 11:14)

V. The Ultimate End of Satan
    A. _____ and _____ (Jude 6; Revelation 20:2–3)
    B. _____ in Hell (Matthew 25:41; Revelation 20:10)

VI. How We Should React to Satan
    A. Don't _____ a foothold (Ephesians 4:27 [NIV]).
    B. _____ against him (Ephesians 6:11–16).
    C. _____ him (James 4:7; 1 Peter 5:9).
    D. _____ from him (2 Timothy 2:26).

Remember, _____ _____ is the _____
(John 14:6); the _____ is a _____ and the father of all
lies (John 8:44).

INQUIRY-ACTION 9.3

INFAMOUS LIARS OF THE BIBLE

Assigned Topic and Reference:	
General Details:	**How Satan Works:**
	The Price to Be Paid:
Lesson to Be Learned:	

INQUIRY-ACTION 9.4

LYING AND HONESTY

Lying Promotes	Honesty Promotes

INQUIRY-ACTION 9.5

MEMORY VERSE CROSSWORD

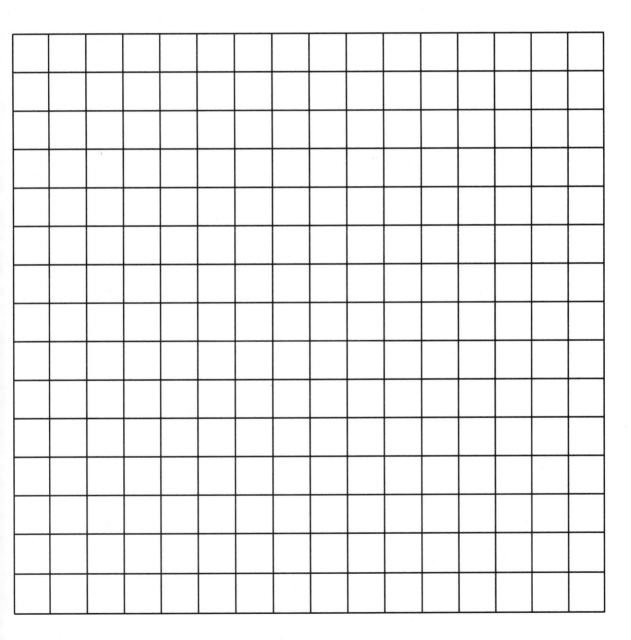

JOYFULNESS

Experiencing Cheerfulness in All Situations

Prisons today are like vacation resorts compared to those in Paul's day. When the Apostle Paul was in prison, he did not have a heated cell with a private toilet and sink. Neither did he have a mattress. There was only the darkness that came with four stone walls, a hard clay floor and no window. And then there was the odor— a stench so suffocating that it could only be that of death!

But the worst part of prison had to be the chains. Paul was constantly bound by heavy chains that tore at his flesh and restricted all movement.

Imagine yourself in Paul's situation. Feel the chains and smell putrid air. Listen to the sounds of others suffering. Search for a ray of light through the cracks. Suppose you were sitting in that prison right beside Paul. What do you think your attitude might be?

In the midst of all of this suffering, the following words are what Paul wrote to his friends in Philippi:

> "But I want you to know, brethren, that the things which happened to me have actually turned out for the furtherance of the gospel, so that it has become evident to the whole palace guard, and to all the rest, that my chains are in Christ; and most of the brethren in the Lord, having become confident by my chains, are much more bold to speak the word without fear" (Philippians 1:12–14).

What an attitude! Rather than being angry about what had happened to him, he was encouraged by the positive impact that his suffering was having upon the lives of others. Paul knew what it meant to experience joy.

Paul did not say that he was happy, for that wasn't true. He wasn't happy to be in prison. He wasn't happy to be separated from the ones he loved. He didn't like being criticized. But he was still joyful.

Happiness relates to outward situations. Joy describes what is within. Joy is the confidence that comes, no matter what the circumstances, because our loving God is in control.

Why was the Apostle Paul joyful? It was because he knew the gospel of Jesus Christ was spreading all over the Roman Empire. Nothing could stop the message that Jesus had died on the Cross for the sins of mankind. Even right there in prison, the good news of Christ had spread throughout the whole palace guard.

Because of Paul's joy even in the midst of suffering, others drew strength to openly stand for the testimony of Christ. This is the type of joy that we should also experience in our lives. Whatever the situation, Jesus Christ should be the Source of our satisfaction.

Sometimes Christians believe that because they have been born again, they won't have any more problems. Then when the problems of life come, they become angry, depressed and even doubtful of God. Being a Christian does not insulate us from problems. In fact, there will be many times that your faith in Christ will cause others to persecute you. That was certainly true of Paul. However, we can experience true joyfulness when we place our confidence in God, no matter what the situation.

What situations in your life right now could rob you of your joy? The prophet Nehemiah said, "Do not sorrow, for the joy of the Lord is your strength" (8:10). Do you believe the words of Nehemiah? In spite of the difficulties you may be experiencing at home, with your friends or at school, do you believe that the Lord can give you the joy and strength to be victorious? He can if you will just tune your heart and listen to Him.

There once was an old rancher who had a violin, but it was badly out of tune. Since he had no way of tuning it out in the desert, he called a radio station and asked them on a certain hour, on a certain day, to strike the note "A." The station decided to grant the old rancher his request. On the particular day that was requested, the true tone of the "A" was broadcast. The old rancher was able to tune his violin, and once again his cabin was filled with beautiful music.

In order for joy to fill our lives, we must be in tune with God. This means that we must be obedient to His Word and in communication with Him through prayer on a daily basis. Joy will only come when we are in a right relationship with our Lord.

As you learn more about joyfulness this week, remember that the Lord is our true source of joy.

"Do not sorrow, for the joy of the Lord is your strength"
(Nehemiah 8:10b).

". . . In Your presence is fullness of joy . . ." (Psalm 16:11).

"These things I have spoken to you, that My joy may remain in you, and that your joy may be full" (John 15:11).

INQUIRY-ACTION 10.1

Happiness

Joy

Definition

Definition

INQUIRY-ACTION 10.2

REASONS FOR JOY

Salvation	Psalm 118:24
Christian friends	1 Thessalonians 2:19–20
The Lord made and controls today.	Philippians 4:1
Being in God's house	Psalm 40:8
Training others to follow Christ	Galatians 5:22
It is commanded.	Luke 2:10–11
God's Word	Jeremiah 15:16
God's Spirit	Romans 5:3–4
Troubles and suffering	Romans 15:13
Obedience	Psalm 122:1
Life of purpose	Ecclesiastes 5:10–20
Hope	John 16:23–24
Answered prayer	Philippians 4:4
Sins are forgiven.	1 Peter 1:3–9
It gives strength and encouragement.	Psalm 16:5–11
Eternal life	Romans 14:17–18
It is healthy.	Psalm 96:11–12
Serving God	Proverbs 17:22
It lasts forever.	1 Peter 4:13
Christ will return.	Psalm 51:7–8
God's Creation	Isaiah 35:10
Continuing presence of God	Psalm 126:5–6

INQUIRY-ACTION 10.3

STUMBLING BLOCKS TO JOY

Stumbling Block 1: 2 Samuel 11; Psalm 32:3–4; 51:3, 12;
1 John 1:8–9; Proverbs 20:11; 29:1

Stumbling Block 2: Philippians 3:1–3

Stumbling Block 3: Hebrews 12:6–11;
(See Ephesians 6:1–2; Hebrews 13:17
and Romans 13:1–5)

Stumbling Block 4: Job 1; 1 Peter 1:6–9; James 1:2–4

INQUIRY-ACTION 10.4

JOY

Diminishers	Enhancers

INQUIRY-ACTION 10.5

PSALM 100

MakeajoyfulshoutforjoyfullynoiseuntotheLordallyoutheyearth
landsworshipservetheLordwithgladnesscomebeforehishim
presencewithjoyfulsongsingingknowyethattheLordhimselfheis
Goditishewhothathasmadeusandnotwearehisourselvesweare
hispeopleandthesheepofhispastureenterintohisgateswithanks
givingandintohiscourtswithpraisegivebethanksthankfulunto
himandblesspraisehisnamefortheLordisgoodandhisloving
kindnessmercyloveenduresisforeverlastingandhisfaithfulness
truthendurescontinuesthroughtoallgenerations.

SELF-CONTROL

Keeping Myself from Thinking and Doing Wrong

What names come to your mind when you study American history? Certainly, you think of George Washington, Thomas Jefferson, Patrick Henry, Abraham Lincoln, Robert E. Lee and many others. But when you think about the men and women who played a part in the development of this great nation, do you think about the pastors and evangelists? These men also shaped the attitudes and beliefs of an entire nation as they faithfully proclaimed the Word of God.

Jonathan Edwards, former president of Princeton University, is regarded as the greatest theologian and philosopher in America's history. But Edwards was more than a scholar. He was a man who applied the teachings of God's Word to his life.

As Edwards was preparing for the ministry, he developed a list of resolutions to live by. When he was finished, his list included a total of 70 resolutions. As you read some of them, remember that he developed his list before he was twenty years old and then lived faithfully by these standards throughout his life.

1. Resolved, "That I will do whatsoever I think to be most to the glory of God . . . ."

2. Resolved, "Never to lose one moment of time, but to use it in the most profitable way I possibly can."

3. Resolved, "Never to do anything which I should be afraid to do if it were the last hour of my life."

4. Resolved, "Never to do anything out of revenge."

5. Resolved, "Never to speak evil of anyone."

Why did Edwards prepare a list of 70 resolutions to guide him through life? It was because he understood what the writer of Proverbs 25:28 meant when he wrote, "Whoever has no rule over his own spirit is like a city broken down, without walls." Edwards knew that man is constantly tempted to do or say things that do not bring glory to the Lord. He knew that the Bible teaches that God can give us the strength to gain self-control over the temptations that surround us. Those who are God's servants must have control over those things that are tempting.

Did you make any New Year's resolutions this year? Have you kept them since the start of the year? Have you ever eaten too much of your favorite food and then immediately said, "I shouldn't have done that"? Have you ever lost your temper and said things that you wish you had never said?

Each time these things happened to you, you probably felt some kind of inner conflict. On one hand, you felt like doing or saying what you did. And on the other hand, you were sorry for what you did or said.

Nobody described it better than the Apostle Paul when he said, "I have the desire to do what is good, but I cannot carry it out. For what I do is not the good that I want to do; no, the evil I do not want to do—this I keep on doing" (Romans 7:18–19 NIV). Paul knew that sin and "the things of this world" would always be there to tempt him to make the wrong choices. He knew that only by God's help could he maintain self-control when he was tempted to do wrong.

Think about the very practical ways that you can demonstrate self-control in your life right now. Are your words "out of control"? If you gossip about others, speak angrily or use profanity—you are out of control! Remember Proverbs 12:18—"Reckless words pierce like a sword, but the tongue of the wise brings healing."

Could it be that your thought life is "out of control"? Do you tell dirty jokes, watch movies or read magazines that show sex or violence? Do you desire possessions that don't honor the Lord? These are characteristics of a mind that is "out of control." In Colossians 3:2 we are reminded, "Set your minds on things above, not on things on the earth."

Do you waste time, fail to plan, or make decisions without thinking of the consequences? Do you spend hours with video games or just goofing off? Are you disorganized or careless? Do you lack purpose and direction? If you do, your life is "out of control." Only God can help you bring your life back under control. Regarding personal self-control, the Apostle Paul said, "See then that you walk circumspectly, not as fools but as wise, redeeming the time, because the days are evil" (Ephesians 5:15–16).

Wouldn't it be great if self-control were as easy as changing channels? You could have one button for "calm down," one for "do your homework," and one for "stop eating." Unfortunately, life isn't that simple. Self-control is not available at the touch of a button.

Self-control comes when we deliberately choose to follow God's teachings and do what is right. The 70 resolutions that Jonathan Edwards wrote were his public testimony of how the principles of God's Word applied in his life.

Do the principles of God's Word control your speech, your thoughts, your actions and your desires? Don't forget, "the fruit of the Spirit is . . . self-control" (Galatians 5:22–23).

Self-control is really a matter of God-control!

INQUIRY–ACTION 11.1

SELF-CONTROL BIBLE STUDY

1. According to Galatians 5:23, we are commanded to have _____ -_____ (temperance).

2. Other Bible words which mean self-control include _____
_____
_____.

3. Check your concordance and give one more reference which indicates we should have self-control.

4. Self-control is a topic that the Bible addresses more in a negative sense, that is, in warnings against foolishness and thoughtlessness (simple mindedness). For each reference in Proverbs, list the traits associated with being foolish or simple. Then use opposites to describe a person with self-control.

Proverbs		Traits of Foolishness	Traits of Self-Control
1:22-26; 3:11-12; 5:12-14; 12:15; 15:12, 32	Knowledge		
6:6-11; 10:4-5; 12:11 and 24; 14:23; 20:4; 24:30-34; 28:19	Self-Control		

INQUIRY-ACTION 11.1 (CONTINUED)

7:6–10, 21–22; 9:13–16; 14:15	10:1; 11:29; 13:1; 15:5 and 20; 17:21 and 25; 19:13; 27:10; 28:7	12:16; 14:16–17, 29–30; 15:1–8; 17:1; 20:13; 21:19; 22:10, 24–25; 27:15–16; 29:9, 11, 22	12:26; 13:20; 18:24; 23:20–21; 24:1
Desires	Relationships	Emotions	Friends

INQUIRY-ACTION 11.1 (CONTINUED)

	Speech — 10:8, 14, 18–19, 21, 32; 11:9, 12–13; 12:18–19, 23; 13:3; 15:2; 17:28; 18:2, 6–7, and 13; 22:23; 29:30		
	Actions — 10:13; 14:9; 22:3; 26:11		
	Life — 12:18; 19:3; 21:21; 22:4		

5. The most important part of this study for me personally is:

_____

6. An area of self-control I would like to see improved this week is:

_____

INQUIRY-ACTION 11.2

STEPS TO BETTER SELF-CONTROL

Self-control is a process. This
means to grow or develop all
my life.

Therefore, I should _____

_____

_____

_____

_____

INQUIRY-ACTION 11.2 (CONTINUED)

**Self-control is a unique challenge
for each person. What is a problem to
one person can be very different for
another.**

Therefore, I should _____

_____

_____

_____

_____

INQUIRY–ACTION 11.2 (CONTINUED)

Self-control depends on sound thinking. The right way to think comes from God's Word.

Therefore, I should _____

_____

_____

_____

INQUIRY–ACTION 11.2 (CONTINUED)

Self-control is really a matter of God's control—bringing every thought and action into obedience to Christ.

Therefore, I should _____

_____

_____

_____

_____

INQUIRY-ACTION 11.2 (CONTINUED)

Self-control is the practice of inner strength—an exercise of my will to do what is right and not do what is wrong.

Therefore, I should _____

_____

_____

_____

_____

INQUIRY-ACTION 11.3

TITUS 2:11–13

LOYALTY

The Bond That Never Breaks

More than at any other time, loyalty is most clearly evident when men and women serve their country on the fields of battle. This was certainly true of U.S. Navy Commander Jeremiah Denton. Commander Denton was flying his twelfth combat mission over North Vietnam on July 18, 1965, when his twin-jet A-6 attack bomber was struck by ground fire.

Commander Denton bailed out of the crippled jet and was immediately captured by North Vietnamese soldiers. His capture marked the beginning of the greatest test of faith, courage and loyalty that he would ever face in his life. For the next seven-and-a-half years, he would be moved from one prison camp to another throughout the country of Vietnam.

Denton was the first A-6 pilot to be captured. Because the plane was new to combat, he expected to be tortured for information about the aircraft that would be of value to the enemy. He was prepared to die rather than reveal any secrets.

As his imprisonment extended from months into years, he was indeed tortured. But the torture was not for the military knowledge that he had. Instead, what the North Vietnamese wanted were statements that would have propaganda value, both with the country's civilian population and with the outside world.

After considerable torture, Denton agreed to a television interview with a Japanese newsman. Of course, this interview was completely controlled by the North Vietnamese. Throughout the interview, Commander Denton calmly blinked his eyes in Morse Code, repeating just one word over and over again: TORTURE—TORTURE—TORTURE.

During the interview, Commander Denton told the newsman that he supported the policies of the U.S. Government. When Naval Intelligence officers saw the film, they were not concerned with the words coming out of his mouth. What they saw was the word TORTURE communicated with his eyes. Commander Denton had given the world the first direct evidence that American prisoners were suffering excruciating pain from beatings and starvation.

Throughout his imprisonment, Jeremiah Denton prayed regularly. He said his prayer time always included at least two things. First, he prayed that he would be able to safely return home to his family. Second, he prayed that God would give him the strength to resist his captors and remain loyal to his country.

His prayers were answered in 1973, when he was released from prison. He not only returned home safely, but he also remained loyal to God and his country while in prison. When he stepped from the aircraft onto American soil, he knelt, kissed the ground and echoed the phrase, "God, bless America!"

Loyalty is a relationship of commitment to someone else. In spite of the difficult situation he faced, Commander Denton remained loyal to his God and his fellow countrymen.

Loyalty is a character trait that is quickly vanishing from our society. People change jobs, spouses, churches and friends with little thought of what it means to break the bonds of these relationships. When the Apostle Paul was imprisoned for his beliefs, Onesiphorus came to comfort him. Although most of Paul's friends had deserted him, Onesiphorus, a runaway slave, risked his life to help him. In 2 Timothy 1:16–17 Paul wrote, "Onesiphorus. . . was not ashamed of my chains; but, when he arrived in Rome, he sought me zealously and found me."

Why do individuals no longer value the importance of loyalty? Do you know people you can count on for loyal support? Can others depend on you to be loyal to them? Most importantly, are you a loyal follower of the Lord Jesus Christ?

The answer to these questions begins with understanding the important principle taught in Luke 14:26: "If anyone comes to Me and does not hate his father and mother, wife and children, brothers and sisters, yes, and his own life also, he cannot be My disciple."

You may have read this verse before and wondered why the Lord said that in order for us to love Him, we must hate our father, mother, wife, children, brothers and sisters. To understand what Jesus was saying, you need to understand that He was using an idiom to emphasize an important principle.

An idiom is "an expression of language that is peculiar to a certain group of people." It was common for the Israelites to express their feelings by the use of a strong contrast. Thus, in Luke 14:26, the word "hate" was used as the opposite of the "love" His disciples should show in their loyalty to Him. Our Lord was not saying that we should have a hateful attitude toward our loved ones. He was saying that our loyalty to Him should be without compromise.

This idea is illustrated in lives of missionaries like William Borden, who gave up his family and untold wealth to serve only a few years on a foreign field. His words challenge us: "No reserves; no retreat; no regrets."

When we proclaim our loyalty to someone, we are saying that nothing will cause us to break our relationship with that person. Unfortunately, too many people enter into a relationship with their own built-in "escape hatch." In other words, if the circumstances surrounding the relationship become too hard to bear, they will be able to escape from their commitment.

For example, many husbands and wives no longer feel an obligation to be loyal to each other. As soon as problems become too great to bear, they obtain a divorce. There are Christians who will freely bear testimony of God's goodness until they face persecution. When the persecution becomes too great, they find an excuse (their "escape hatch") to desert their Savior.

Upon turning the leadership of Israel over to Joshua, Moses said, "Be strong and of good courage, do not fear nor be afraid of them, for the Lord your God, He is the One who goes with you. He will not leave you nor forsake you" (Deuteronomy 31:6). Jesus, our Perfect Example of loyalty, said, ". . .lo, I am with you always, even to the end of the age" (Matthew 28:20b).

It is our responsibility to be loyal in our relationships to others, as well as in our relationship to God. But real loyalty will only happen when you are willing to lock your personal "escape hatch" and throw away the key!

Are you willing to make that decision today? Jesus will always be loyal to you. Will you always be loyal to Him?

INQUIRY-ACTION 12.1

PLEDGE ALLEGIANCE TO FRIENDS

Ideas to include:

_____

_____

_____

_____

_____

_____

_____

_____

_____

_____

_____

_____

I Pledge Allegiance to My Friends

_____

_____

_____

_____

_____

_____

_____

_____

_____
signed

INQUIRY-ACTION 12.2

PLEDGE ALLEGIANCE TO FAMILY

Ideas to include:

_____

_____

_____

_____

_____

_____

_____

_____

_____

_____

_____

_____

_____

_____

_____

_____

_____

_____

I Pledge Allegiance to My Family

_____ signed

Inquiry-Action 12.3

Philippians 3:12–14
Use the verbs as a help in writing the verses.

Not _____ attained

_____ perfected;

_____ press on,

_____ may lay hold _____

_____ has also laid hold _____ .

_____ do not count

_____ to have apprehended;

_____ do, forgetting

_____

_____ reaching forward _____

_____ are ahead,

_____ press toward _____

_____

_____ .

INQUIRY-ACTION 12.4

COMMITMENT TO LOYALTY

If I am loyal to _____**, I will:**

_____

_____

_____

_____

_____

_____

_____

_____

_____

_____

_____

_____

_____

_____

_____

_____

_____

_____

_____

_____

HUMILITY

The Mind of Christ in Us

Some words are hard to define. The character trait "humility" is a good example.
How would you describe a humble person? Is it someone who is soft-spoken?
Does it mean that you always do what others tell you? Or is humility a pattern of
behavior that cannot easily be defined?

Sometimes when it is difficult to define a word, it is a good idea to study a word
that is the opposite of the one you are trying to understand. Although humility is
difficult to describe, its opposite is easy to identify. The opposite of humility is
PRIDE!

Pride began with Satan when he rebelled against God. Satan's rebellion is recorded in Isaiah 14:12–15. As you read the following passage, identify the five "I wills"
declared by Satan (called Lucifer).

"How you are fallen from heaven, O Lucifer, son of the morning! How you are cut
down to the ground, You who weakened the nations! For you have said in your
heart: 'I will ascend into heaven, I will exalt my throne above the stars of God; I will
also sit on the mount of the congregation On the farthest sides of the north; I will
ascend above the heights of the clouds, I will be like the Most High.' Yet you shall
be brought down to Sheol, To the lowest depths of the Pit."

Pride can best be described as an attitude of "I will" or "Me first!" Pride is a self-
centeredness that is at the heart of sin. A prideful person is not content with current position or possessions. The prideful person wants to have more than anyone
else. Sometimes we say that people are proud of being rich, clever or good-looking.
But truthfully, they are proud of being richer, more clever or better looking than

someone else. Pride is believing that you are better than others. Therefore, you believe you deserve the best, the most, and special privileges above the rules meant for others.

Pride is the opposite of humility. It is just like a fire. If you let it start in your life, it will consume you. The book of Proverbs reminds us that there is no place for pride in the heart of the Christian. In fact, God says, "Pride and arrogance . . . I hate" (Proverbs 8:13).

Why are we warned so strongly against pride? Proverbs provides several reasons:

• With pride comes conflict: "By pride comes nothing but strife" (13:10).

• With pride comes punishment: "Everyone proud in heart is an abomination to the Lord; though they join forces, none will go unpunished" (16:5).

• With pride comes shame: "When pride comes, then comes shame" (11:2).

• With pride comes destruction: "Before destruction, the heart of a man is proud" (18:12).

When you got up this morning, did you "put on" humility? That's how the Apostle Peter describes the Christian's daily responsibility. "Yes, all of you be submissive to one another, and be clothed with humility, for 'God resists the proud, but gives grace to the humble'" (1 Peter 5:5). Just as we put on our favorite items of clothing, we should also clothe ourselves with humility every day.

Humility is thinking about others and not about ourselves. The humble man never thinks about his humility. In fact, the humble man does not think about himself at all. It's not that he thinks himself worse than others—unworthy and unuseful. He simply thinks of himself less often. He is not the center of attention.

In spite of all of her fame, the great African-American concert soloist, Marian Anderson, was gracious and kind to everyone she met. She was a beautiful model of humility. One day a reporter was interviewing Miss Anderson. He asked her to name the greatest moment in her life.

There were many people in the room that day. They knew of the many accomplishments of Miss Anderson. Among themselves, they were guessing which event she would choose as the most important in her life. Would it be the time that she gave a private concert at the White House for the Roosevelts, who were entertaining the King and Queen of England? Would it be the time she became a delegate to the United Nations? Or would she choose that Easter Sunday in Washington, D.C. when she stood at the Lincoln Memorial and sang for a crowd of 75,000—a crowd that included Cabinet members, Supreme Court Justices and most members of Congress? There were so many memorable events in her life. Which one would she choose?

Miss Anderson quietly told the reporter that the greatest moment of her life was the day she went home and told her mother she wouldn't have to do other people's laundry to make a living anymore.

Many people would not want the whole world to know that they were from a poor family. Somehow we believe that others would think less of us if we tell the truth about our background. So instead of clothing ourselves with humility, we pretend to be someone we really aren't. As a result of pride, we put on different "masks" to hide who we really are.

Are you hiding behind a mask of pride today? It might be that you are a good athlete, and you are proud to be better than everyone else. Or it might be that you are attractive, and you are proud to be better looking than everyone else. Your pride might come as a result of your family's wealth or your grades in school. As long as there is an attitude of pride in your life, you will not be able to clothe yourself with humility. Remember, the blessings that you have are not a result of something you have done. Your abilities, the way you look and your family environment are all gifts from God.

Being humble doesn't mean that you let everyone tell you what to do. It doesn't mean that you're not good at something or shouldn't strive to do your best. Humility means respecting others and appreciating their talents, while remembering God as the source of your own. Humility also means being willing to admit that someone else can do something better than you can. A humble person will often step out of the way and give someone else the opportunity to succeed.

Is there pride in your life? Are you willing to take the necessary steps to remove your pride and show humility in your attitude and behavior? These seven steps will help you as you seek to honor the Lord through a humble attitude:

1. Spend time meditating on God and His Word. (Psalm 119:9–16)

2. Do not focus on your needs, but on the needs of others. (Philippians 2:3–8)

3. Admit your faults. (James 5:16)

4. Submit to those in authority over you. (Ephesians 5:21)

5. Resist the desire to praise yourself. (Proverbs 27:2)

6. Do good deeds privately. (Matthew 6:1–4)

7. Show kindness to everyone. (Matthew 5:43–47)

INQUIRY-ACTION 13.1

A WARNING AGAINST PRIDE

Luke 18:9–14	For those who are proud of their physical ability
1 Corinthians 1:30–31	For those who are proud of their wealth
1 Corinthians 4:6–7	For those who are proud of the way they look
Hosea 10:13	For those who are proud of their intelligence
1 Samuel 16:7	For those who are proud of their spirituality
Psalm 49:10–12	For those who are proud of their talents
Ecclesiastes 5:19	For those who are proud of their work
Jeremiah 9:23	For those who are proud of their service to God

INQUIRY-ACTION 13.2

THE HUMILITY OF JESUS

Luke 2:8–20   Jesus' humble _____

Luke 2:2:41–52   Jesus' humility before _____
                          _____ and _____

Matthew 3:13–17   Jesus' humility in _____

Luke 4:1–15   Jesus' humility in _____

John 13:1–5   Jesus' humility before _____
                          _____

Matthew 7:1–5;   Jesus _____ about
Luke 6:27–42; 14:7–14 humility.

Luke 23:26–46;   Jesus' humility in _____
Philippians 2:8

INQUIRY-ACTION 13.3

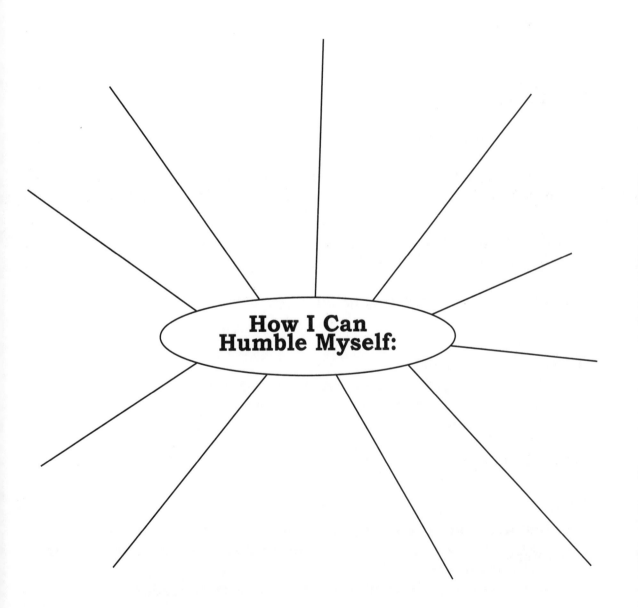

How I Can
Humble Myself:

Inquiry-Action 13.4

Humbling Ourselves Before God

Opening Paragraph:
- An interest-grabbing question
- A clear statement of the purpose of your essay

Second Paragraph:
- The meaning of humility
- The meaning of its opposite: pride

Third Paragraph:
- Why being humble is important
- Include three or four reasons.
- Include the dangers of pride.

Fourth Paragraph:
- Practical suggestions for showing humility
- List, then weave together your ideas.
- Other paragraphs can be added if you want to have one for home or family, one for school or friends, etc.

Fifth Paragraph:
- Restate again the main reason for humility's importance.
- List steps to its growth (see the final section in your text for Chapter 13).
- Write a closing sentence to encourage your reader.

INQUIRY-ACTION 13.5

1 PETER 5:5–6

all	older
and	one
another	opposed
are	opposes
at	people
be	proper
because	proud
but	resisteth
clothe	resists
clothed	same
due	subject
elder	submissive
elders	submit
exalt	that
for	the
gives	therefore
giveth	those
God	time
God's	to
grace	toward
hand	under
He	unto
humble	up
humility	way
in	who
is	with
likewise	yea
lift	yes
may	you
men	young
mighty	younger
of	your
	yourselves

CONFIDENCE

Trusting What God Has Said

It all started over four thousand years ago in a region known as Ur of the Chaldees. Ur was a large, wealthy pagan city located southeast of what is now Baghdad.

There were many rich, influential men in the city. One of them was named Abram. But like many other things in his life, even his name would soon change. Of all the men living on the earth at that time, God chose to deliver a clear, life-changing message to Abram. "Get out of your country, from your family and from your father's house, to a land that I will show you. I will make you a great nation; and I will bless you" (Genesis 12:1–2).

That was quite a promise that God made to Abram, especially when you consider that Abram (to whom God gave the new name Abraham) was already an old man when the promise was given. Remember, he was 75 years old and his wife Sarah was 65 years old. They had no children, yet God promised to give them a son whose offspring would be as numerous as the stars of the sky (Genesis 15:5). For a childless couple past the age of normal childbearing, it took a lot of confidence for Abraham and Sarah to believe God's promise.

At the time of life when most couples would be thinking about retirement—a rocking chair on the front porch and a little peace and quiet—Abraham and Sarah had to think about getting a rental truck and new furniture for a nursery. Think about it! Abraham had never before heard the voice of God who had called him. He did not have a Bible to give him directions. All he knew about this God came from the stories passed down from the days of Noah. Yet he believed God and confidently began his journey to Canaan.

We have so many more reasons to have confidence in God today. From the Bible we learn more about God than Abraham could have ever known. It is through His Word that we become acquainted with God's plan, promises and prophecies. When we study history, we cannot help but see the thousands of proofs of the Bible's authenticity.

Did you know that there are over 300 prophecies in the Old Testament about the Messiah? The following are just a few examples:

- Hundreds of years before Jesus' birth, His birthplace was named (Micah 5:2).
- King Herod's massacre of boy infants was foretold (Jeremiah 31:15).
- The escape of Joseph and Mary with the baby Jesus into Egypt was predicted (Hosea 11:1).
- Jesus' suffering, death and burial were accurately described (Isaiah 53:4–12).
- His resurrection was proclaimed centuries in advance (Psalm 16:8–11).

Back to the story of Abraham:

In the years that followed, Abraham's and Sarah's confidence in God grew as they watched Him fulfill the promises He had made. Throughout their journey from Ur to their new home, God protected and provided for them. Although it was 25 years before the promised son was born, God kept His word.

And what about God's promise that Abraham's offspring would be as numerous as the stars? The nation of Israel and the Jewish people are living proof that God keeps His promises. Because God is always truthful, we can have complete confidence that He will do as He says.

Our faith is not rooted in theory, speculation or hearsay. It is based on facts. Our confidence comes as a result of Who God is and what He has done. The record of God's marvelous works is recorded in His Word.

Our confidence in God can be strengthened as we follow the pattern set forth by Abraham. To begin with, we must believe God's Word completely. When God spoke to Abraham and told him to leave Ur of the Chaldees for another country, Abraham did not go home to talk it over with others and decide if that was a good idea. Abraham immediately began to make preparations to leave. Based on what God had done in the past, Abraham was confident that God would provide for the future.

There are other examples of those whose confidence increased because they believed God's Word completely. When the Israelites said they couldn't conquer Canaan because of the strength of the people who lived there, Caleb "answered the people . . . and said, "Let us go up at once and take possession, for we are well able to overcome. The Lord is with us. Do not fear them'" (Numbers 13:30, 14:9).

When David faced Goliath and the armies of the Philistines (1 Samuel 17:32–51), he was confident that God would give him the victory. When Daniel would not bow down to pagan gods and was cast into the lions' den (Daniel 6), he was confident that God would bring deliverance. Hebrews 11 gives other examples of men and women whose confidence grew stronger because they were willing to believe and follow God.

Time after time the Bible describes men and women who believed God's Word completely. As a result of their belief, they were ready to confidently take the next step: They followed God's Word completely. The formula for confident living is illustrated by the many examples found in the Bible. Believe God + Follow God = Confidence.

Have you ever taken the time to think about how God has kept His promises in your life? Spend a few minutes reliving the past victories that God has given you. Look at a photo album, review your diary or talk to your parents about how God has worked in your life and the life of your family. You will soon realize how God has faithfully led you every step of the way.

True confidence can only be found in God. Our God is faithful. What He promises, He will fulfill. When we faithfully follow Him, we can be confident that we will be victorious.

INQUIRY-ACTION 14.1

LIFE

The Wrong View	The Right View

With God's help, I want to be _____

_____

_____ .

Date _____

INQUIRY-ACTION 14.2

REASONS BIBLICAL CHARACTERS COULD ACT WITH CONFIDENCE

1. _____

_____

2. _____

_____

3. _____

_____

4. _____

_____

5. _____

_____

The lesson for me is: _____

_____

_____.

INQUIRY-ACTION 14.3

BUILDING CONFIDENCE

Knowing God's nature gives me confidence.

Knowing God's purpose and plan gives me confidence.

Knowing God's love gives me confidence.

Knowing God's direction and power gives me confidence.

Inquiry-Action 14.4

Hebrews 13:5b, 6, 8

For He Himself has said,

"_____

_____."

(Deuteronomy 31:6)

So we may boldly say:

"_____

_____

_____?"

(Psalm 118:6)

_____   _____

_____ , _____

and _____.

ORDERLINESS

The Pattern for Successful Living

After an eleven-hour flight from Europe, the jumbo jet landed safely at 10:32 A.M. Although the passengers of Flight #68 were tired from the long trip, it had been an uneventful journey. In just a few more minutes the plane would park at the gate, passengers would get their luggage and then be on their way home. Or at least that's what they thought.

Nothing seemed out of the ordinary until the plane approached the terminal. Gate 14 was their destination. As they approached, there was no one on the ground to guide the pilot. So they waited.

Finally a man with the company's uniform and sound mufflers on his ears appeared. He seemed surprised that the plane was waiting to taxi to the gate. He hurriedly took his place and guided the pilot to his final parking spot. The passengers thought they were home at last.

The passengers gathered their belongings from the overhead racks and waited patiently in the aisles for the forward door to open. After a long delay, the pilot announced over the intercom that no one had brought the stairway to the plane's door. They had to keep the door closed until it was safe to exit.

Finally the stairway appeared, and the passengers left the plane. It was now more than an hour since they had landed. The delays caused by the airline's personnel had put all of them in a very bad mood. All the passengers wanted to do was get their luggage and GO HOME!

But their ordeal was not yet over. All of the signs to the baggage claim area had been taken down to be repainted. There were no temporary signs to guide them. It seemed to take forever to get directions.

When they arrived in the baggage claim area, the passengers looked for their flight number on the screens above the carousels so that they would know where to find their baggage. But since some of the screens were not working, they could not find their flight number.

They finally learned that their luggage was to arrive on the first carousel. As their baggage arrived, the passengers quickly realized that some pieces were missing. On his way to file a report for his missing piece, one passenger noticed it on the next carousel. Soon the other passengers discovered their luggage on different carousels. Although they had been told that it would arrive on the first carousel, the luggage appeared on all eleven of the airport's baggage carousels.

As the passengers of Flight #68 left the airport, they had already forgotten the good memories of their trip to Europe and the flight home. All they could think about was the "airport nightmare" they had just experienced. Now that they were outside of the terminal and on their way to the parking lot, they wondered if this nightmare would continue.

Whether or not the nightmare continued is another story. The difficulties the passengers had experienced would not soon be forgotten. The lack of organization by airport and airline personnel had made the final moments of the trip miserable for the hundreds of passengers on Flight #68.

The Apostle Paul knew the importance of orderliness when he wrote in 1 Corinthians 14:40, "Let all things be done decently and in order." Paul not only knew that God was a God of order but also that maintaining order was necessary for successful daily living.

Throughout the Bible, God demonstrates that He is a God of order. In the story of the Creation (Genesis 1:1–2:3), He began with the creation of the heavens and the earth. Then day by day He added to the beauty of His world by creating morning and evening, water, the sun and moon, plants, animals and finally, man.

God's order is also seen in the organization of the Ten Plagues described in Exodus 7:14–12:30. Because Pharaoh refused to let the people of Israel leave Egypt, God brought punishment upon the country in the form of ten plagues. If you carefully study each of the plagues, you will see God's orderliness demonstrated in the way they were organized.

As each plague occurred, the suffering and loss experienced by the Egyptians increased. For example, the first four plagues were extremely unpleasant, but none brought great suffering. But the fifth plague (cattle disease) caused great loss to the Egyptians. The sixth plague (boils) inflicted terrible suffering. The seventh (hail) and eighth (locusts) also brought great loss to the Egyptians as they saw their crops destroyed. The ninth plague (darkness) had a serious psychological effect. After all of their misery, the Egyptians experienced complete darkness in the middle of the day.

In God's organization of the plagues, He saved the most serious punishment until last. The tenth (death of the firstborn) took the lives of the family legal heirs. For the first time, loss of life actually occurred.

Our God is a God of order. Even in the punishment of a nation God had an orderly plan of action. Throughout both the Old and New Testaments, God's orderliness is demonstrated. As a result of God's orderliness, there are two important principles that we should learn.

First, because our God is a God of order, He has a plan for our lives. He wants each of us to know and follow the plan He has set for us. Proverbs 3:5–6 reminds us, "Trust in the Lord with all your heart; and lean not on your own understanding; in all your ways acknowledge Him, and He will direct your paths." God desires that we follow the path He has planned for us.

Second, because our God is a God of order, He expects us to conduct our lives in an orderly manner. This means that God expects us to set goals in our lives and develop plans to reach those goals. Have you developed plans to achieve a closer relationship with God? To become a more successful student? To be more cooperative and helpful at home?

After setting goals, it is important to have a daily plan. Have you made your plan? Are things in order for you to accomplish your plan?

One of the most important characteristics of a successful person is orderliness. With God's help, you can transform those unorganized areas of your life.

The Apostle Paul always wanted to do his best for the Lord. That's why he said in Philippians 3:14, "I press toward the goal for the prize of the upward call of God in Christ Jesus." Setting goals, making plans and doing things in an orderly way, honors the Lord. Are you willing to press toward that mark? The time to begin is now!

INQUIRY-ACTION 15.1

GOD'S SYSTEMATIC ORDER

1. Genesis 1:1–26 _____

2. Genesis 6:11–22 _____

3. Exodus 7:14–12:30_____

4. Exodus 18:13–27_____

5. Exodus 20:1–17_____

6. Judges 7 _____

7. 1 Chronicles 28:12–20 _____

8. Esther 5:1–8; 7:1–6 _____

9. Luke 9:1–6; Luke 10:1–12 _____

10. Matthew 26:17–19 _____

11. Acts 13:4–5; 14:26–27 _____

12. Romans 10:9–10 _____

13. Colossians 3:18–20 _____

14. 1 Corinthians 12:27–28; 14:29–33 _____

15. 2 Peter 1:5–7 _____

16. Revelation 21:9–23 _____

INQUIRY-ACTION 15.2

BENEFITS TO BEING ORGANIZED AND THINGS BEING IN ORDER

1. _____

   _____

2. _____

   _____

3. _____

   _____

4. _____

   _____

5. _____

   _____

The lesson for me is: _____

_____

_____

_____

_____

INQUIRY-ACTION 15.3

SUGGESTIONS FOR ORDERING MY SPACE

1. _____

_____

2. _____

_____

3. _____

_____

4. _____

_____

5. _____

_____

The lesson for me is: _____

_____

_____

_____

_____

INQUIRY-ACTION 15.4

SUGGESTIONS FOR ORDERING MY TIME

1. _____

_____

2. _____

_____

3. _____

_____

4. _____

_____

5. _____

_____

The lesson for me is: _____

_____

_____

_____

_____

Inquiry–Action 15.5

1 Corinthians 14:33 and 40

Draw a line from brick to brick to identify the words of the verses in order, then write them below.

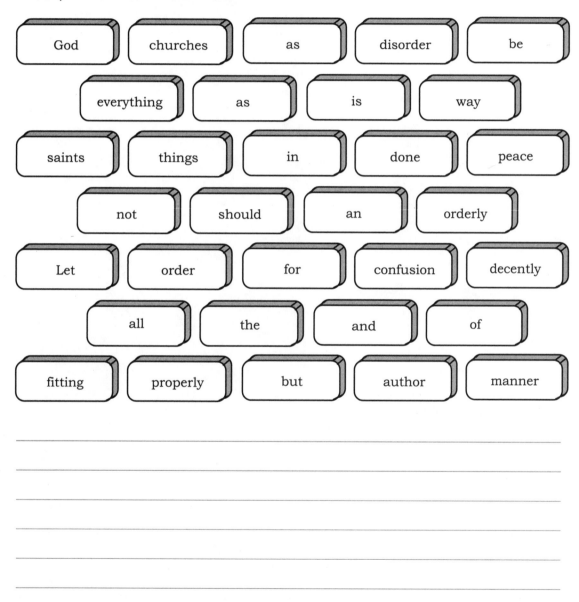

_____

_____

_____

_____

_____

DILIGENCE

Working Hard Until the Task Is Done

For many of us, the most important parts of a journey are the start and the finish. Yet the part of a trip that really tests the strength of a traveler is neither the beginning nor the end, but the many miles in between.

Anyone can be excited at the beginning of a journey, and that excitement will always return when the end is in sight. But it is on those miles in between that the traveler learns the true meaning of diligence.

This is true of all of life's journeys. One day a little boy will hear a great musician and is inspired to begin his musical career. Years later he appears in concert for the first time, and the audience loves him! Overnight he becomes famous. Both milestones, his start and his success, are reported in the papers. Nothing is reported about the many years between his first music lesson and his debut on stage. Nothing is said about all of those years he practiced alone or wanted to quit. But it was not his concert that made him famous. It was his diligence over the years. It was his unwillingness to quit.

There are hundreds of true stories of men and women who have learned the lesson of diligence. One of the most famous stories is that of a young man who was fired from his job at the age of 22. He then went into business with a partner, but the business lasted less than a year. He tried politics but was defeated twice. He finally won a legislative seat but quickly lost it in the next election.

He hoped for a political appointment by his party, but it never came. His girlfriend left him. He had a nervous breakdown. He tried three more political campaigns and lost them all.

At the age of fifty-one, after years of defeats and failures, he was elected President of the United States. His name was Abraham Lincoln. He was a man who knew the meaning of the word "diligence."

The Bible gives many examples of those whom God has blessed as a result of their diligence. Moses is a familiar example to all Christians. Repeatedly he went to Pharaoh and demanded that the Israelites be allowed to leave Egypt for the Promised Land. In spite of Pharaoh's refusal each time Moses came to him, Moses would not give up. Finally the people were set free.

Moses' diligence did not end there. He now had the responsibility to lead the Children of Israel to the Promised Land. Under normal circumstances, this trip would not take too long. But because of their sin, the Israelites would wander in the wilderness for the next 38 years. During all of this time Moses was their leader. It was because of his diligence that the people were finally allowed to enter the land God had promised to them.

Diligence is a character trait that is not commonly found in people today. For most people when a task becomes too difficult, they give up. Instead of sticking to the task until it is done, they quit. Then they try to justify their actions by offering excuses: "It was too hard." "I wasn't interested anyway." "You didn't explain it to me properly." "That's not my responsibility."

Do you want to be successful in life? Certainly you do! But success will never come if you are not diligent in the tasks set before you today. Remember, if you allow yourself to quit once, it will become much easier to quit the next time you face a difficult challenge.

Stop for a moment and think about the tasks that you have to complete every day. Every student has the responsibility to do homework and to be prepared in class. Many students have some type of daily practice for music or sports. Most students have assigned chores to do at home each day. Other students help with the family business.

Now that you have identified tasks that you are responsible to complete each day, consider the following "diligence principle" taught in Galatians 6:9, "And let us not grow weary while doing good, for in due season we shall reap if we do not lose heart."

In this verse the Apostle Paul reminds each of us that if we are diligent in our responsibilities today, God will bless us in the future. The pathway to future success is sticking to today's tasks until they are done.

No matter what age you are, there will always be obstacles that stand in the way of completing a task. Today visiting with your friends at the mall or on the telephone might be your excuse for not completing a task. When you are grown, a television program or responsibilities at work might be your excuse.

The majority of people seek the "easy way out." It is always easier to blame something or someone else for our failure to do what we are supposed to do. A true test of our character comes when we complete a task no matter how hard or distasteful it may be.

Think about all of the things you have to do this week. Based on your past experiences, which of those tasks will you find the most difficult to complete? Ask the Lord right now to give you the diligence necessary to finish those tasks.

Remember, there is nothing so fatal to character as half-finished tasks! Be known as someone who will always get the job done. "And whatever you do, do it heartily, as to the Lord and not to men" (Colossians 3:23).

INQUIRY-ACTION 16.1

GOD'S PERSPECTIVE OF WORK
Write two references to support each principle below.

1. God instituted and commanded work.

   _____   _____

2. Jesus had work to accomplish.

   _____   _____

3. Enjoyment and success in our work comes from God.

   _____   _____

4. The purpose of work is to provide for life's needs.

   _____   _____

5. All work is to be done as unto the Lord.

   _____   _____

6. Laziness must be avoided.

   _____   _____

7. God gives eternal rewards for our work.

   _____   _____

Inquiry-Action 16.2

Diligence "Flow Chart"

Look up the following passages of Scripture as you complete the chart.

Reference:	How diligence is demonstrated:	Personal benefit:
Hebrews 11:6		
Matthew 5:13–16		
1 Timothy 2:1		
Matthew 28:19–20		
2 Timothy 2:15		
Luke 19:11–27		

Inquiry-Action 16.3

The Diligence of God's Servants

Assignment: _____

Scripture: _____

1. What are the main points of this story?

2. How did God's servant demonstrate diligence?

3. In what way did God show His blessing?

4. Plan for presentation:

INQUIRY-ACTION 16.4

WHAT DOES IT TAKE TO STOP YOU?

I want to . . .	I may be stopped from achieving my goal because . . .	I will do the following to overcome this/these obstacle(s) . . .
1.		
2.		
3.		

Remember: It is no disgrace to fail, but it is a disgrace to do less than your best to keep from failing.

INQUIRY-ACTION 16.5

COLOSSIANS 3:17 AND 23 (NKJ)

Add all the two- and three-letter words to complete the verses.

_____ whatever _____ word _____ deed, _____

name _____ Lord Jesus, giving _____

thanks _____ Father through _____ .

_____ whatever _____ , _____ heartily, _____

Lord _____ . . . .

PRAYER

Experiencing God's Power Made Available to Us

Jesus, when talking to His disciples, said, "When you pray...," not "If you pray...." There is a big difference. Jesus expected his followers to be men of prayer. Prayer was to be a natural and regular means of communication between man and God.

In today's society, prayer is not seen as a natural response to God, but as a "religious observance" that should only be done in church or in the privacy of your own home. That is not what God desires from His people. He desires for us to talk to Him with the same ease and trust that was demonstrated by police Sergeant Felix Jimenez in the following story.

The headline "Diver Recovers Cockpit Voice Recorder from ValuJet Crash" in *The News Herald* (May 27, 1996) did not tell the whole story. Following is the actual account as reported by Lisa Holewa from *The Associated Press*.

MIAMI - A police homicide sergeant searching the murky waters where ValuJet Flight 592 crashed into the Everglades found the crucial cockpit voice recorder Sunday afternoon.

The voice recorder could provide clues as to why the DC-9 crashed May 11, killing all 110 people aboard.

"When we stopped for a break, I said, 'God, so far I've just prayed for you to keep everyone safe out here and I haven't asked for your help finding anything. Now I'm asking you to help us find this recorder,'" said Metro-Dade Sgt. Felix Jimenez.

"The next time I put my probe into the water, it hit the recorder," Jimenez told The Associated Press.

"Authorities packed the recorder in a water-filled cooler to keep the tapes from drying out and shipped it to National Transportation Safety Board headquarters in Washington for analysis," said NTSB spokesman Mike Benson.

The testimony from Sgt. Jimenez is clear: God does hear and answer our prayers. It may not always be as quick and dramatic as described in this story, but the prayers of God's people will not go unanswered.

What keeps you from regularly praying to God? Are you concerned that you are not using the right kind of words? Does your posture make a difference? Do you always feel like you are asking for something when you pray?

The answers to many of our questions about prayer can be found in Matthew 6. In verses 5–8, Jesus does not tell His disciples that their prayers must use a "special" language or that praying must be done on bended knees. What Jesus does say is that when we pray, we should not be doing it to impress others with how spiritual we are.

Beginning with verse 9, Jesus taught the disciples what has commonly been called "The Lord's Prayer." For centuries Christians have memorized this prayer and recited it both privately and in public places. When this prayer of Jesus is prayed, God is honored.

Jesus said in verse 9, "In this manner, therefore, pray." The purpose of The Lord's Prayer was to show the disciples that prayer does not just consist of asking for things. From The Lord's Prayer, we learn that there are five different aspects of prayer.

The first aspect of prayer is **adoration**—praising God for who He is. The Lord's Prayer begins, "Our Father in heaven, hallowed be Your name." Through these words, Jesus reminded the disciples and us that we are not praying to one of the many false gods worshipped by the pagans. The God to whom we pray is the Ruler of all of Heaven, the One whose name is holy in all the earth. Our initial approach to God when we pray is to praise Him for who He is.

In verse 10 Jesus prays, "Your kingdom come. Your will be done on earth as it is in heaven." Through these words, Jesus reminded His disciples that God is in control of all things. As a result, prayer should include **appreciation** for God's blessings to us and care for us.

The third aspect of prayer is **supplication**-—telling God about our own needs. In verse 11 Jesus said, "Give us this day our daily bread." It is the "asking for things" that most people think of when they think of prayer. What most people don't understand is that our focus should be on our needs, not our wishes. Although there are many things that we would like to have or like to happen in our lives, our supplication should be about those things that will honor Him.

Confession is admitting our sin to God and asking for forgiveness. It should be a part of every prayer. Jesus gives us the example in verse 12: "And forgive us our debts, as we forgive our debtors." Not only should we ask God to forgive us of our sins, we must forgive others of the wrongs they have committed against us. In the same way we seek God's mercy, we must extend it to others.

The final aspect of prayer is **intercession**—asking God to act in our behalf and in the behalf of others. Verse 13 says, "And do not lead us into temptation, but deliver us from the evil one . . . ." Jesus knows that in this world there are those who not only hate God, but also hate those who love God. Only God can provide sufficient protection for the Christian against the power of Satan in this world. As we offer intercessory prayer, we acknowledge the danger and the power of God to give us the victory.

Do your prayers sound something like this? "I need your help, Lord. I know I haven't talked to You for a long time, but if You will only do _____ for me, I'll go to church every Sunday, quit lying, be nice to my sister, _____." Sound familiar? Just fill in the blanks with your latest crisis and promise.

God doesn't specialize in quick fixes or granting wishes like a magic genie. But He does care deeply for you, and He does answer prayer. Our prayers aren't just "wish lists" or speeches. Instead prayer is intimate conversation with God. It is sweet, quiet communication. You can tell Him what's on your mind, confess sins and thank Him for everything!

Jesus prayed frequently and has instructed us to do the same. Now is the time to begin a regular conversation with your Heavenly Father. Take time right now to communicate with Him through prayer. Follow the pattern that Jesus set in The Lord's Prayer. What He taught His disciples was meant for you as well.

INQUIRY-ACTION 17.1

MATTHEW 6 — THE MODEL PRAYER

Verse   9 _____

Verse 10 _____

Verse 11 _____

Verse 12 _____

Verse 13 _____

Inquiry-Action 17.2

Prayer Diary

Date: _____

Prayer Request:

_____

_____

Date: _____

Answer to Prayer:

_____

_____

Date: _____

Prayer Request:

_____

_____

Date: _____

Answer to Prayer:

_____

_____

Inquiry–Action 17.2 (CONTINUED)

Prayer Diary

Date: _____

Prayer Request:

_____

_____

Date: _____

Answer to Prayer:

_____

_____

Date: _____

Prayer Request:

_____

_____

Date: _____

Answer to Prayer:

_____

_____

INQUIRY–ACTION 17.2 (CONTINUED)

PRAYER DIARY

Date: _____

Prayer Request:

_____

_____

Date: _____

Answer to Prayer:

_____

_____

Date: _____

Prayer Request:

_____

_____

Date: _____

Answer to Prayer:

_____

_____

Inquiry-Action 17.2 (CONTINUED)

Prayer Diary

Date: _____

Prayer Request:

_____

_____

Date: _____

Answer to Prayer:

_____

_____

Date: _____

Prayer Request:

_____

_____

Date: _____

Answer to Prayer:

_____

_____

INQUIRY-ACTION 17.3

TYPES OF PRAYER

____ 1. Psalm 67:3

A. Confession—admitting our sin to God and asking for forgiveness.

____ 2. Psalm 100:4

B. Appreciation—thanking God for the blessings He gives.

____ 3. Daniel 9:4–5

C. Supplication—telling God about our needs.

____ 4. Ephesians 6:18

D. Adoration—praising God for Who He is.

____ 5. Philippians 4:6

E. Intercession—asking God to act in the lives of others.

INQUIRY-ACTION 17.4

PERSONAL PRAYERS

In order to improve your understanding of the five types of prayers, write your own short prayer for each type listed below:

A prayer of adoration: _____

_____

_____

_____

A prayer of appreciation: _____

_____

_____

_____

A prayer of supplication: _____

_____

_____

_____

A prayer of confession: _____

_____

_____

_____

A prayer of intercession: _____

_____

_____

_____

INQUIRY-ACTION 17.5

HEBREWS 4:15–16 (NKJ)

All vowels and spaces have been omitted from the words in the verses. Replace them along with all the punctuation, and write the verses below.

FrwdnthvHghPrstwhcnntsmpthzwthrwknsssbtw snllpntstmptdswrytwthtsnLtsthrfrcmbldltththr nfgrcthtwmybtnmrcndfndgrcthlpntmfnd

REVIEW

Highlights of *CharacterQuest*

Character has many different names. At home, it is love. In business, it is honesty. At play, it is fairness. Whatever its name, the highest and noblest aspects of character are always found in the life of the Lord Jesus Christ.

The reason that Jesus is our role model for character is that His life on earth bore testimony to what He believed. He lived outwardly exactly as He thought inwardly. We cannot say that we have noble values and then act in an ignoble way. What we say we believe and how we conduct our lives must be consistent.

Developing the highest values and then living according to those values have been the focus of our study during these past weeks. Matthew 7:24 reminds us of the importance of the Biblical principles presented in this text, "Therefore whoever hears these sayings of Mine, and does them, I will liken him to a wise man who built his house on the rock." Read the verse again, placing the emphasis on "hears" and "does" as Jesus taught.

Remember, every person is the architect of his or her own character. Each of us is like a building contractor. Only it is not a shopping mall, an office building or a house we must construct. Our responsibility is to build our own character. Let's take a brief look at the highlights of each of the character building blocks studied this semester.

Building Block 1: LOVE—The Foundational Character Trait

There are two types of love: conditional and unconditional. Most people love with a conditional love—a love based on "if you will do something for me."

Jesus loves us with an unconditional love. He loves us "no matter what." Unconditional love is the foundation of all character development.

Building Block 2: WISDOM—Knowledge Used for God's Glory

The Word of God always distinguishes between knowledge and wisdom. Knowledge refers to learning facts or information. Wisdom refers to the practical application of knowledge to life opportunities. For the Christian, wisdom is using knowledge for God's glory.

Building Block 3: OBEDIENCE—Always Doing What God Says

Obedience begins by recognizing who has legitimate authority in our lives. Although there are many individuals who have authority over us, God is the ultimate authority in our lives. Obedience, whether to God or another authority placed over us, is not an option. God's blessing will come to those who obey immediately and completely.

Building Block 4: COURAGE—Unafraid to Follow God

Courage is not the absence of fear. Courage is being aware of the dangers, but going ahead anyway because of the importance of what must be done. It's impossible to live victoriously for Christ without courage. Talk is cheap—action requires courage! Christians must be people of courage, unafraid to follow God.

Building Block 5: ATTENTIVENESS—The First Step to Success

How many times have you done something wrong or gotten into trouble because you failed to pay attention? Listening carefully to others is a very valuable lesson to learn. However, the most important type of listening is hearing the voice of God through His Word, prayer and godly counselors. Attentiveness is the first step to success with God and with others.

Building Block 6: FAITH—Acting on God's Promises

There are two types of faith: saving faith and walking faith. The Christian life begins with saving faith (John 3:16). After this first step, our walk with God begins

(1, 2, 3 John). Christianity demands faith—the ability to act on God's promises as recorded in His Word.

Building Block 7: RESPONSIBILITY—Demonstrating Reliable Conduct in Every Situation

When it comes to responsibility, there are those who accept responsibility and those who run from it. God desires to entrust each of us with opportunities to serve Him, but these opportunities will only come after we have demonstrated that we are responsible individuals. Are you willing to take personal responsibility for your actions by doing what you need to do? If so, God will bless you and use you in ways you could only dream of.

Building Block 8: THANKFULNESS—An Attitude of Gratitude to God

What would it be like if you lived in a culture whose language did not include the words "thank you"? Everyone has a reason to be thankful. Expressing thanks should not be a once-in-a-while event. Thankfulness should be a part of everything we do, every day. Our lives should be characterized by "thanks-living." In all things we should have an attitude of gratitude to God.

Building Block 9: HONESTY—Always the Best Policy!

If your life is not characterized by honesty, it is characterized by dishonesty! There is no middle ground. In John 14:6 Jesus is described as "the Way, the Truth and the Life." If we call ourselves followers of Jesus Christ, then we must be honest in all things. Don't be fooled! Honesty is always the best policy.

Building Block 10: JOYFULNESS—Experiencing Cheerfulness in All Situations

Sometimes Christians believe that because they have been born again, they won't have any more problems. Then when the problems of life come, they become angry, depressed and even doubtful of God. For these people the source of joy is "things." We can never experience happiness in all situations until we learn that the true source of joy is the Lord.

Building Block 11: SELF-CONTROL—Keeping Myself from Thinking and Doing Wrong

Most people have a control problem. For some, their words are out of control. For others, their thought life is out of control. There are those whose lives are out of control. God reminds us that one of the fruits of the Spirit is self-control (Galatians 5:22–23). Self-control comes when we deliberately choose to follow God, keeping ourselves from doing wrong.

Building Block 12: LOYALTY—The Bond That Never Breaks

Loyalty is a commitment to someone else. It is a relationship that is maintained no matter how difficult the situation may become. As people continue to change jobs, spouses, churches and friends, loyalty vanishes from our lives. Jesus, our Perfect Example of loyalty, said, ". . . lo, I am with you always, even to the end of the age " (Matthew 28:20). The bond of loyalty between our Savior and us will never break. In turn we should be loyal to our family and friends.

Building Block 13: HUMILITY—The Mind of Christ in Us

Humility is a difficult word to define. Yet when compared to its opposite—pride— the meaning becomes clear. A humble individual realizes that all abilities and possessions are gifts from God. Humility is also the willingness to admit that someone else can do something better than you can. When we give God the glory in all things, the mind of Christ is in us.

Building Block 14: CONFIDENCE—Trusting What God Has Said

From Abraham, to the Apostle Paul, to current-day believers, the lives of men and women have been changed for eternity because they had confidence in what God said. Our faith is not rooted in theory, speculation or hearsay. It is based on facts. Our confidence comes as a result of trusting what God has said. When avoiding pride and emphasizing self-confidence, we can live without anxiety because we are assured of God's power, presence and protection.

Building Block 15: ORDERLINESS—The Pattern for Successful Living

Throughout the Bible, God demonstrates that He is a God of order. His organization is seen in the story of creation, the organization of the exodus from Egypt and the feeding of the 5,000. As a result of God's orderliness, there are two important principles to learn. First, He has a plan for our lives and desires that we follow the path He ordains. Second, He expects us to conduct our lives in an orderly manner. God knows that orderliness is the pattern for successful living.

Building Block 16: DILIGENCE—Working Hard Until the Task Is Done

Diligence is a character trait that is sadly lacking in people today. When a task becomes too difficult, most people give up. There is an important "diligence principle" in Galatians 6:9: "And let us not grow weary while doing good, for in due season we shall reap if we do not lose heart." The pathway to diligence is working hard and sticking to today's tasks until they are done.

Building Block 17: PRAYER—Experiencing God's Power Made Available to Us

A prayer is not a religious speech for others to hear or a "wish list" of things you would like to have. Prayer is intimate conversation with God, telling Him what's on your mind, confessing sins and thanking Him for everything! Jesus prayed frequently and has instructed us to do the same. Through prayer God's power is made available to us.

You are the architect of your character. The decisions that you make today shape your future. These 17 building blocks will make a difference in your life for eternity.

INQUIRY-ACTION 18.1

REVIEW IT OR LOSE IT

Character trait: _____

Key verse: _____

Definition: _____

_____

Biblical example/story illustrating this character trait:

_____

_____

Three important facts I have learned about this character trait:

1) _____

2) _____

3) _____

The main reason students do not demonstrate this character trait in their lives:

_____

_____

Example of how this character trait can be demonstrated in my life:

_____

_____

INQUIRY-ACTION 18.2

REVIEW IT OR LOSE IT

Character trait: _____

Key verse: _____

Definition: _____

_____

Biblical example/story illustrating this character trait:

_____

_____

Three important facts I have learned about this character trait:

1) _____

2) _____

3) _____

The main reason students do not demonstrate this character trait in their lives:

_____

_____

Example of how this character trait can be demonstrated in my life:

_____

_____

INQUIRY-ACTION 18.3

FINAL COMMITMENT

Your paper will not be seen by anyone except you. Your honesty will allow God to work in you as you develop godly character.

* The one truth from this course that has been most important to me is:

  _____.

* A character trait which I feel confident in is:

  _____.

* The character trait that needs most improvement is:

  _____.

* The biggest obstacle to my improving this area is:

  _____.

* Some things I want to work on are:

  _____

  _____.

* I want to commit myself to developing godly character.   Yes ❑   No ❑
  If yes, complete the next page.

INQUIRY-ACTION 18.4

Commitment to Character

Based on the challenges presented in this course, I am willing to commit myself to the development of godly character. I understand that this includes both believing and doing the right things based on God's Word.

Signed: _____

Dated: _____

"Delight yourself also in the Lord, and He shall give you the desires of your heart." (Psalm 37:4)